The
Secret Rules
of
Successful
Marketing

Research to Riche$:

The Secret Rules of Successful Marketing

Welcome to the secret world of marketing research

Jim Nelems

Published by
LONGSTREET PRESS
2974 Hardman Court
Atlanta, GA 30305

1st printing 2002

ISBN: 1-56352-709-X

Contents

The Use and Importance of Marketing Research

There are as many different definitions of marketing research as there are trade and professional associations and authors. Many people who do or think they do marketing research are not actually conducting research as most of us would think of it, and many if most "marketing research" firms do far more research than "marketing" research without giving it a second thought.

Marketing research (and it is marketing research not market research!) can be as narrow or as focused as determining the color and typestyle for a label of dishwashing detergent, or as broad based as determining the television viewing habits of over 200 million households. It can help shape the design of a new dog biscuit or shape the opinions—and thus actions—of the nation's leaders.

Although people were asking questions and doing what we now call "polls" as early as 1824 (in a straw poll for President in Wilmington, Delaware) long before most people had heard of marketing research, it was with the advent of mass marketing (mass production and mass advertising) that true marketing research as we know it today, began. Many people credit Charles Parlin of Curtis Publishing *(Saturday Evening Post)* with popularizing marketing research through his magazine readership studies over fifty years ago.

The real "hero" in marketing research, however, which most younger researchers may well have never heard of, was a German physicist turned author, Alfred Politz, who after arriving in the U.S. in 1937 not only developed but set the standards for valid and reliable marketing research for over 25 years—especially in the areas of advertising testing and media readership studies. It was Politz who said, back in 1937, that the purpose of advertising is not to get people to remember the **advertising** but to remember the **brand.** Today one can easily see that many advertisers have totally forgotten his words because they create *advertising* to be remembered instead of the *brand* to be remembered.

Whether a company is a large multi-national corporation or a small corner market drug store or car wash, there is room for sound marketing research in helping to make the business grow and prosper by answering such questions as:

— What is the size of the market for my product
   or service?
— Who am I competing with?
— What sizes, shapes, flavors, and attributes should
   my product or service have?
— What kind of advertising should I do, to whom,
   what should the ads be saying?
— How much money should be spent on advertising,
   and where?
— What prices should I charge?
— Where is the market going in the future?
— How should my product be positioned in
   the marketplace?

— What should the advertising say?
— Where and how should my product be sold?
— What do my prospects and customers think
  of my products?
— How do I know if my marketing program
  is successful?
— How do I know how to change and move
  onto something else?

It is marketing research which helps answer these types of questions. Marketing research is the systematic review, collection, processing, and analysis of information related to how to more effectively perform marketing functions.

But good researchers do more than marketing research. They do public opinion and public issue research. They do employee attitude research. They do social and psychological research.

Although this book will focus on marketing research, whatever type of research, be it marketing or another type, the same rules, warnings, procedures, and cautions are warranted. A bad questionnaire design, a poor sampling plan, erroneous data processing or poor analysis will affect any type of research project, and no more (or less) for marketing research than any other type of research.

A. Quick Primer for the Non-Researcher

Marketing researchers, as do most professionals, have a language all their own, which may not be totally understood by non-researchers. We often use the same words, but with different meanings; for example, "universe" which does not mean that, but rather the base from which a sample is drawn, also known as "population," which can mean more than what most people think of as the human population.

As an overview, marketing research is generally discussed in two different dimensions:

1) **Qualitative versus quantitative.** The first dimension is related to the size of the sample in the study, either **qualitative** (small sample) or **quantitative**

(large sample). There are no rules as to what sample size fits what category, but generally samples less than 100 are considered qualitative and those over 100 quantitative. Qualitative is also used in another dimension associated with small samples, and that is to say research that is **diagnostic**— or the reason "why" rather than **evaluative** (how many). Focus groups are the best (or worst) examples of this.

2) **Primary versus secondary research.** The second classification is whether the researcher collects the numbers directly, called **primary** research, or through **secondary** research, which consists of reviewing what others have done. Curiously, one usually does secondary research first, and primary research second.

Primary research is then generally classified with regard to the technique used, that is to say how the data is collected. Data can be behavioral, observational, or attitudinal. There are four data collection techniques: (1) personal interviews (which can be in variety of locations, such as in a shopping mall, on site at the client's place of business, at home, or elsewhere) (2) telephone, (3) mail (or faxed) surveys, and (4) electronic. Internet surveys are the most common electronic method of data collection, but many "data mining" programs collect sales and other data without the use of human intervention and must be counted here.

Many of the problems in marketing research arise out of these classifications: using the wrong technique for the wrong reason, doing one type (qualitative) but treating it as the other (quantitative).

Typically, marketing research is conducted by specialized marketing research firms or by research departments within companies who typically go through the marketing research companies for at least some part of the research process. There are about 7500 entities in the United States who identify themselves as "marketing research firms," in addition to the thousands of other companies such as advertising agencies and consulting firms who either do the research themselves or contract it out to research firms.

The expansion of the Internet has opened up the industry to many other parties who claim to conduct marketing research, and more and more people are doing, or would like to do, their own research.

It's certainly possible to do your own research, even if you are not a trained marketing researcher, and there have been several good books written on this. The question is, however, if one's time might be better spent in managing the business, and calling in professionals for specialized services like marketing research, accounting, and advertising. Any further comment on the wisdom and value of using an outside marketing firm might be considered biased, since the author owns a marketing research firm, so I will leave it at that.

Now, on to the methods and meaning of marketing research, so we can see how much fun it is.

The Methods of Marketing Research

1.

Not everything called marketing research is really marketing research.

Marketing research is often a catchall category whenever anyone is referring to collecting and reporting facts, opinions and attitudes. But just because someone calls something marketing research does not mean that it really is marketing research—or valid marketing research, which is the critical issue. Call in polls, push polls, sugging, and frugging do not deserve to be called marketing research.

"Call-in" polls aren't marketing research. That's where a TV station (usually) posts two phone numbers on the screen and says dial this number if you are in favor of the question and that number if you are against it. In the course of an evening, they might have 23,000 people who call in and vote their opinion, usually in a simple yes or no. And how can 23,000 answers be wrong? After all, most polls only survey 900 to 1000 people or less.

In most cases, the 23,000 people **are** wrong, as far as projecting the data. Yes, there are 23,000 people who expressed their opinion (say, 18,000 said yes and 5,000 said no). But this is a "self-selecting" sample. Only those who felt strongly enough about the issue took the time and effort to call. And in virtually every case, the people who feel strongest are the ones calling in. The best example of this goes back to the early days of call-in polls, where then-Alabama Governor George Wallace won every call-in poll ever conducted for president that year. George had a lot of friends and supporters, but they did not represent a cross-section of the voting public.

Ted Turner used to do a lot of call-in polls on his Superstation Channel 17. Ted spoke at an American Marketing Association meeting one year and took questions from the audience. Someone said, "Mr. Turner, why do you do these call-in polls? You know they are not a scientific sample of the public."

In typical fashion, Ted replied. "Hell, yes, I know that, but what the heck, we get a million dollars a year from our call-in polls."

As a footnote, I am happy to report that the Turner Foundation, in which Ted Turner and Jane Fonda have played key roles, later sponsored some of the most significant research ever conducted on teen pregnancy, which led the Georgia state legislature not to adopt a new law that, by eliminating sex education below the ninth grade, would have increased teen pregnancies. We know this because of a statewide poll conducted at the time; it had such a large sample of teenagers the researchers were able to break out girls who had, versus did not have, sex education below the ninth grade, and thus could show statistically that teens who had such education had fewer pregnancies than those who did not. Having confidence in the poll, and in Jane Fonda presenting it, caused the legislators not to tamper with the law.

"Push Polls" are not marketing research. A push poll is a relatively new phenomenon, used only in political elections. A "push poll" is called that because the true purpose is not to solicit opinions, but rather "push" the respondent towards a particular candidate by giving, or at least implying, negative information about the poll sponsor's opponent. Such a survey may start off like a regular poll and may sound like a legitimate survey, but it then veers into territory most researchers don't want to go. Under the guise of asking questions, the "interviewers" are really imparting or "pushing" negative information about the candidate meant to influence opinions and later voting intentions. While the objective of a push poll may be stated as trying to find out what issues people really care about for a particular candidate, and where that candidate might be vulnerable, the reality is that it is really telemarketing, or campaigning, in disguise. Here is a real example:

> "If you heard that John Brown (candidate for Congress, fifth Congressional district) had recently been arrested for beating his wife,

would that make you more or less likely to vote for him?"

Sometimes the questions are very close to a real life event. Perhaps the candidate had been arrested or charged with beating his wife. But actually, whether or not John Brown has in reality been arrested is irrelevant. For if you call 20,000 people and ask them that question, then you have provided negative information to 20,000 people in that voting district.

There are at least two tip-offs that this is a push poll. The first is the question itself, framed the way it is. However, some of the questions may not be as obvious as "beating his wife" or "charged with fraud." What if the question is "opposed to affirmative action" or "arrested for drunken driving?" Maybe that's a legitimate question to ask and the candidate himself wants to know if it affects his chances.

The second tip-off, even more difficult to determine, is the number of people "surveyed." A typical political poll might involve perhaps as many as 800-1000 interviews (most local candidates can't spend much money on marketing research). So if a "poll" is conducted to many thousands of people in a concentrated area, coupled with the type of question above, then it is likely to be a push poll. Researchers, who are the only ones who would know how many people would be surveyed, must decline doing push polls because it's the right thing to do.

While push polls in politics are a recent event, this technique is not new to marketing research. Many years ago a major automobile manufacturer conducted what today would be called a push poll. In this instance, researchers surveyed thousands of people over the country, but instead of giving negative information, they provided the respondents with a whole series of positive pieces of information about the automobile make. The reading of a series of 12-15 positive statements about the make in question was not intended to get agreement or disagreement about each of the statements but rather to communicate these 12-15 product benefits about the brand.

"Sugging and frugging polls" are not marketing research. Sugging means "Selling Under the Guise of Research." Sugging is using what appears to be a poll or survey, when the purpose is really to sell a product. Here is a typical sugging example. A magazine publisher sends out a mailing to subscribers saying that, as a valued reader, they want the reader to "test" a new publication. It will be sent free, and all you have to do is fill out a survey and tell them what you think. Sounds OK so far. But here's the kicker. Buried later in the fine print, at the end of the letter and in the request card the reader sends in, is this comment:

> "We are so sure you will like this new magazine that we will enter your subscription to it. Then, if you decide you don't want it, you can write and cancel your subscription." (Sounds like they have already done the research, doesn't it?)

Although the publisher, a well respected name in publishing, would no doubt defend this as a legitimate research study (they would probably say that the number of people who fail to cancel is the real test of whether or not it will succeed) is there anyone who really thinks this is anything other than an attempt to sell magazine subscriptions under the guise of research?

Frugging means "Fund Raising Under the Guide of Research." Most people in this country have received many "surveys" asking for their opinions, along with a request for a contribution, which, contrary to what the mailing says, does not go to "processing the data" but rather goes directly to the fundraiser. Objective political surveys should never ask for a donation to process or report the findings. And of course, even if the findings were reported, no one would pay any attention to them because all politicians know the truth about these "polls."

Here's an example of a typical frugging question:

"The federal government is trying to (INSERT ONE OR MORE OF THESE ACTIONS) take away our right to own a gun/make it possible to kill innocent babies/keep teenagers from having adequate sex education so that unwanted children will be born who we will all have to pay for. Most people think this is wrong. How do you feel? And send $7.00 to process your answers, so we can send the results to the Senate and House of Representatives."

Maybe they tabulate the data and send it in. I don't know. But I happen to think that our senators and representatives are smart enough to know what to do with this kind of information. Consider the source. Ever seen an organization reporting data detrimental to its cause? You don't have to hide data to keep this from happening. Just make sure you ask the questions the right way to get the answer you want.

The Council of American Survey Research Organizations (CASRO) has taken a strong lead in publicizing these mis-uses of marketing research, but there are so many of them now, CASRO doesn't even bother. But frugging apparently still works, and they will continue to flood the mails—and probably the Internet in the future.

None of this is illegal, but it is annoying and lowers the reputation of marketing research.

Many polling opportunities posted on the Internet and available to the casual web surfer are not marketing research. Some organizations have simply replaced the "call in" telephone poll with questions posted on the Internet, available to anyone who happens to access their website. Such polls can create a false conclusion as to what the general public thinks. Just because someone can post a survey question on a website, does not mean that they should, or that it is a representative sample of opinions. It may be entertainment, but it is not scientific research.

It is possible to "rig" an Internet poll, through "electronic ballot stuffing." As reported in *The New York Times*, a particular photo contest, which had been receiving about 50,000 votes per week, suddenly received five million votes in which most of those votes turned out to be a different pattern from earlier votes. The contest was suspended when it was learned that e-mails from partisans had gone out encouraging people to vote a particular way, to make a political statement.

Each year, *Linn's Stamp News*, a weekly newspaper for stamp collectors, asks readers to vote for their favorite U.S. postage stamps. The poll for 2001 stamp issues allowed readers to mail in their ballots or send them in over the web. Due to a concentrated campaign by several political organizations, the web survey produced tens of thousands of votes for a particular stamp, which was virtually never selected in the mailback survey. Linn's reported both surveys, but stressed that the web survey was invalid due to "stuffing the ballot box."

It is important, however, to differentiate between Internet polling as described above, and truly legitimate polling over the Internet through the use of panels and other "opt-in" polling opportunities. There are hundreds, and thousands, of such legitimate polls, in which

respondents have been recruited to become members of
Internet panels and agree to answer questions from time
to time. For example, college students who have agreed
to be a part of panel might be e-mailed questions about
their product preferences while away at school; a service
provider may post questions on their website regarding a
purchased product or service; a state tourism commission
may post questions to those hitting their website to find
out what types of activities the potential visitor is interested in, perhaps to know what type of information to
provide. As long as the user of these polls understands
their limits and projectability, and uses them for the purpose they were intended, so be it.

In addition to research that is not really research,
there are the "near misses," or the techniques that
sound like marketing research, and have their place, but
are not marketing research the way most of us think
of it.

One of these techniques would be "comment
cards," the cards left in hotels and restaurants so if you

have a problem or compliment, you can write it down and send it in. Now, these tools are important if you want to correct guest problems in your establishment. And they are also inexpensive to instigate. But since only about 2-5% of guests ever fill them out, and since when they do it is mostly a negative response, they are generally only good at responding to particular situations, such as "the TV remote does not work in room 216." You would be remiss if you thought comment cards are the only way to do real customer satisfaction research. Do it, but know its limitations.

One of these limitations is the method of rèturning the comment card. If you write down a negative comment, be sure to mail it in, rather than leaving it in the room or on the table, or depositing it in a box on the premises. Otherwise, how do you know the person who receives the card actually turns it in? If you were the desk clerk at a hotel, and a guest turned in a card to you that said the desk clerk was unfriendly, what do you think you would do with that card—hand it in to the manager?

Another "near miss" would be the unsolicited mail survey sent to be public at random without a "relationship." Not many of these are done any more because of inherent problems, but they do exist. The reason an unsolicited mail survey of this type is not real research is, again, due to the low response rate. The lower the response rate, the less sure we are that those who respond are typical or representative of those who do not respond.

Many years ago the Georgia Department of Agriculture was involved in a legal battle regarding the definition of a Vidalia onion, which is an onion grown in a particular geographic area in Georgia where the longitude and soil conditions impart a certain taste. In this case, a Texas onion grower had shipped Texas sweet onions into the Vidalia, Georgia area and packaged them in bags saying "from Vidalia, Georgia." To supposedly show that the public was against such a practice, the state printed a short questionnaire in a free publication, the Georgia Consumers and Farmer's Bulletin, which was mailed to over 300,000 households in

Georgia. (One is naturally curious how a Farmer's Bulletin might have a circulation of that magnitude in Georgia, but I digress.)

The question went something like this:

"Would you buy a product called a Vidalia onion if you knew it was really grown in Texas?"

Now what would you expect Georgia farmers to say? They said exactly what you might think. Some 97% of those who paid their own postage to mail in the ballot said they would not buy such a product. In attempting to introduce this survey into evidence at the upcoming trial of the onion grower in Statesboro, GA, the state's district attorney assigned to the case pointed out that these replies were surely valid because they were based on about 2400 replies. And that the sample error on that sample size would be less than 1%.

When the researcher hired by the onion grower was able to speak, he pointed out that the 2400 replies

represented only a 3/4 of 1% response rate of the distribution to over 300,000 people, so there was no indica-
tion at all that the 2400 who *did* reply could be judged
representative of the 298,000 who *did not*. Further, the
wording of the question was easily seen to suggest a particular answer, as well as calling into question to whom
the survey should have been directed in the first place,
onion buyers instead of onion growers. And lastly, one
might question whether the respondents to be interviewed should be farmers, rather than the consuming
public who buys (rather than grows) onions.
Consequently, the study was not admitted into evidence.

(As an interesting side note, the grower was found
not guilty of counterfeiting onions in his trial. Not
because of any research that was, or was not done, but
because there was no law at the time that made it illegal
to sell counterfeit onions. Now, there is, which is how
Vidalia Onions got their trademark.)

Another "near miss" would be the surveys sometimes printed in the Sunday paper in the FSI (Free

Standing Insert) sections. There might be a whole page of questions asking about usage of particular brands. In reality, those running these "surveys" are not really interested in what product you use except as a means to develop a mailing list for their clients. If you say you use Crescent Cleaner, for example, the maker of the competitive brand Terrific Cleaner will mail you a coupon.

Just because somebody asks questions, or collects data, does not mean it is real marketing research.

2.

You can get different conclusions depending upon the research technique you use.

Not enough is said about proper research techniques. There are dozens of ways to conduct research: in shopping malls, over the phone, through the Internet, exit interviews in stores, surveys to members of a mail panel, mail surveys to specific groups, focus groups, etc. And which technique you use can have dramatic results, because different techniques have different response rates, different kinds of people responding, and thus different conclusions which may be drawn.

For example, say you own a bank or restaurant and want to measure your customer opinions. What better and more inexpensive way to do this than to stand in the bank or restaurant and intercept people when they leave? Well, whether or not you should do this depends upon what you want to find out. If you stand in a restaurant and ask opinions, you will get mostly positive ones, because if a person had previously had a bad experience there, it is not likely he would come back, meaning this person would not be in the restaurant to be interviewed. You have a skewed sample, skewed in the sense that you have a higher concentration of heavy users. If a person eats there daily, she is seven times as likely to be interviewed than someone who eats there once a week. And since heavy users tend to be more favorable (otherwise they would not be heavy users), you overstate the positive opinions of the restaurant. You end up getting a sample of positive respondents, especially because they all know you are being paid to do the survey for the sponsor, and people generally like to be pleasing if they know who is paying for the research.

Nevertheless, there are some types of data that are perfectly fine to collect on premise, even opinions of the restaurant, as long as you also do "neutral research," such as a random phone survey where the respondent does not know the sponsor to find the guests of your restaurant as well as those of the competition. And even opinions on-site are OK as long as you are comparing them in certain ways: for example, comparing opinions of customers of each location versus one another, or comparing opinions of younger versus older customers, or comparing to see if customers in a given territory or in a particular franchisee have different opinions from their counterparts.

Be aware that not all demographic groups respond equally to different techniques. Mail surveys will generate a higher response rate among older people than among younger ones, so don't use a mailback survey to measure customer demographics unless you have data to make the proper adjustments.

Surveying the wrong people can hurt you. The most famous example of this is the often-quoted demise of the

Literary Digest magazine back in 1936 because their polling incorrectly predicted that Alf Landon would defeat Franklin Roosevelt for the presidency, by a 59% to 41% preference for Landon. When the final results were tallied, the findings were almost exactly the reverse: Roosevelt got 61% of the vote and Landon only got 39%. As it turned out, for many years including during the 1936 election, the *Literary Digest* mailed a ballot to potential voters using a list of people who owned an automobile and had a telephone. In the past, the fact that the survey voters owned a car or had a phone made no difference in how they voted. But in 1936, still in the depression, it did. The voters who received and returned the ballot were mostly Republicans, while most of the people who actually voted in the election were Democrats.

Interviewing at different times of the day or week can impact results. If you do a telephone poll all in one day, you obviously don't have the opportunity to reach people not at home on that day. And since younger adults go out more than older ones, you miss the younger sample. Some research firms used to adjust for "not-at-homes" by asking people when they were most likely to be away from home, but people won't answer that question any more due to security reasons. (Why do I need to tell the interviewer when I am not home, unless he is going to come back and rob my house while I am not there?)

Even changing the time of day of the interviewing can make a big difference in results. One company used to use an outside marketing research firm to do its customer satisfaction research but felt it would save money by hiring its own retired employees to conduct the telephone interviews. The outside research firm had been conducting the interviews six days a week, from 10 am to 9 pm local time. Under the new system, however, the retired employees came into the company's office and used the company's call center from 9 am to 5 pm, Monday-Friday. (They did not work at night or on Saturday when they were a full time employee, and they were not going to start now!) Also, the corporate office building's heat and air conditioning was turned off at 6 pm, so it was uncomfortable to work in the evening.

The results of a simple change in the time of day dramatically affected the customer satisfaction ratings. The ratings changed: not because customer satisfaction had changed, but because the customers who could be reached Monday-Friday between 9 am-5 pm were not representative of their total customer base. Eventually, the company abandoned its in-house call center and went back to outside research providers.

3.

Most people won't talk to you if you are doing a survey.

S ad, but true. A few years ago, telephone surveyors could count on completing interviews with up to 65% or so of all the people they got on the phone. Now, the latest data show that about 30-35% of consumers contacted by phone will talk to you. This means that most of the opinion polls conducted in this country are based on a minority of those contacted who provide their opinions.

And it's true for shopping malls as well. Research firms get reports from mall interviews showing how many people were approached for the survey, how many refused, how many qualified to be interviewed, etc. However, most of the time, these reports don't show the "wave-offs." A "wave-off" is a unique marketing research term: it means all the people whom you **started** to approach in the mall, but the potential survey participant used his or her hand to wave you off, to keep you from approaching close enough to even ask if they could be interviewed.

And even this 30-35% (for telephone surveys) is misleadingly high, because it counts only the people you talked with and ignores all those homes with Caller ID (11% and growing), those where you could never get through on answering machine (over 60% of homes have an answering machine and multiple calls have to be made to reach them), busy signals, and other numbers which may be (but which you may not know) data lines, fax numbers, and cell phone exchanges. It's not uncommon in a survey where you have completed 800 interviews to have gone through 10,000 phone numbers.

There are many reasons for a low response rates today. First, it's not the topic matter, although we have seen reports that people will tell you anything on the phone as long as you don't ask about any guns in the home. And we do know, from several studies, that men will tell you—whether it is true or not—how many times they have had sex with a prostitute, and women will tell you how many times they have been the victim of spousal abuse (5.4% in the last twelve months according to one statewide survey), even down to the type of weapon used: gun, knife, fists, etc.

In most cases, the refusal rate has little to do with what the topics you are surveying: whether you want to ask questions about personal products, lingerie, incontinence, or male impotence (but thanks to Bob Dole for introducing the more user-friendly term ED). In fact, most refusals come before the prospective respondent even knows the topic.

Other factors than the topic of the survey are at work here. One is our society and the way we are all moving, thanks to PC, the Internet, and the number of hours we work today. We are all so busy, or at least we think we are so busy, that we don't want to spend any "unnecessary time" answering those long, boring, and silly survey questions. "What's in it for me?"

Today, most adults under age 65 work outside the home, so obviously most survey calls need to be made in the evening, starting around dinnertime. Back 20 to 30 years ago, most calls—at least those to women—were made during the day. Housewives were considered the primary target audience for most consumer products, and since housewives by definition were at home, what better time to reach them?

Many marketing researchers think the main reason for the decline in the co-operation rate is "those pesky telemarketers." After all, there are over 500 million tele-marketing calls made each week.

Timeout: the industry distinguishes between "tele-marketing" calls and "research" calls, and so do the state and federal governments. A **telemarketing** call is defined as a call where the purpose of the call is to moti-vate the recipient to take a certain kind of action: usually this action is to buy something, or in the case of political telemarketing calls, to vote for a certain candidate or to contribute to a certain charity or political organization. If you answer a certain way, you will have agreed to take a specific action: buy a product, attend a meeting, order something by phone, etc.

By contrast, a **research** call is defined as a call in which the aggregate opinions of the persons called are solicited. Your name will never be given out, and your opinions will only be used in combination with others. You will never be asked to buy anything or to take any specific action.

Unfortunately, to many consumers, these are all the same types of calls. They are calls by (in many cases) a company the consumer has never heard of, at the same time of day, and the caller is taking a lot of the consumer's time in asking the various questions.

Not only that, some telemarketers try to disguise themselves as "taking a survey," when the only "survey" they are really doing is a "survey" to find out how many people are interested in what they have to sell. This is now illegal, but such automates have not stopped. So it's not difficult to understand that many people do not make the industry distinction.

Further, from a market researcher's standpoint, there is a difference in attitude between interviewers and telemarketers. Since telemarketers are generally paid on the basis of how much business they bring in and therefore someone who is not a good prospect is really wasting their time, they often care little about whether or not the recipient of the call is treated nicely. As soon they find out the person is not a prospect, many telemarketers will immediately hang up and go on to the next person.

By the way, you can tell if you are about to be the recipient of a telemarketing call, many of which are automated now. If you answer the phone after one ring, and there is no one on the line immediately, but rather some kind of buzzing or humming sound, or silence, that's a telemarketing call. The telemarketer has set the automatic dialers to dial numbers faster than a human voice can answer; your phone has been switched to a station so a person can talk with you, but there is no one yet at that station. Just hang up. We suspect that telemarketers have a different view of the two industries than do market researchers, which is probably one reason why firms tend to do either telemarketing or marketing research, not both.

Speaking to the relationship between marketing research and telemarketing, a large marketing research firm, purchased several years ago by a large telemarketing firm, eventually sold its newly acquired marketing research division to another marketing research firm. Seems that telemarketers and marketing researchers simply can't work together. Just because both use telephones in their work does not mean compatibility.

A recent trend, however, is for marketing researchers to now use automated calling and ask the questions to whomever answers the phone, either by using voice recognition or by using instructions such as "press one for yes, or two for no." You can see many potential problems with this, including whether or not the person who answers the phone is really qualified to do the study, either by age, residence, or meeting category qualifications. Another real problem is that it reduces all questions to a simple multiple choice, when in fact often people don't have an opinion.

A recent automated poll, for instance, asked this question:

"Do you think the new Northern Arc highway should be built? Say yes or no."

Even assuming that everyone asked this question knows what the Northern Arc highway is, which is a big assumption in itself, there are many other problems with this question. Many people in the survey area may be undecided on this issue and simply can't say yes or no at this point. However, if you say, "don't know," the same computer voice asks the question again, and if you do not say yes or no, the recipient gets a quick computer generated voice: "Thank you for your opinion" and a hang up. It's problematic whether or not, or how, the computer counts a no response to this question.

Fortunately for marketing researchers, by law, legitimate survey researchers are excluded from virtually every law that regulates or bans telemarketing calls, because telemarketing calls are legally defined as above. But that does not keep the person whose dinner is interrupted from thinking it is all the same thing, and this is one factor that has reduced co-operation in survey research. When a surveyor calls and the respondent thinks the survey call is a violation of the Telemarketing Fraud Act, it does little to increase co-operation for the interviewer to say, "Actually Mr. Jones, this is a survey and is not a telemarketing call, therefore we are not in violation of the law." This only makes it worse.

Recently CASRO proposed a program to help improve the image of marketing research, and thereby to increase the response rate to surveys, and thus lower the cost of data collection. However, nobody wanted to pay for such a program, given reasonable estimates of how much it would cost and how long it would have to be in place.

While no industry initiative will likely come to pass, the individual client and the research firm can do their part to increase the public's survey response rate. It's really very simple: well-trained professional interviewers, interesting, easy to understand—and to answer—questionnaires, telephone interview lengths no greater than 15 minutes, and respect for the individual.

When we have a client who won't complete a pilot questionnaire of his own design because his questionnaire is too long, we know we still have a long way to go.

4.

The size of the population has nothing to do with how many people you need to interview.

Even though research is pretty well accepted today, there are substantial portions, at least of the general public, who have a general misconception or lack of understanding as to how sampling works. That's why you often hear comments such as these:

"They have never called me on a poll."

"How can 600 people represent 100 million?"

"If you are going to do a national sample, you need to talk with more people than if you want to just interview in Iowa."

It seems logical that if you want to be more accurate, you should talk to more people. And if the size of the population is larger, it again seems logical that you should have a larger sample. But these are simplistic statements with only a grain of truth in them.

It is true that as you talk to more and more people, you increase accuracy of a survey. But accuracy is not proportionate to sample size. For example, if you double the sample size, you only increase the accuracy by 50%. You reach a point of diminishing returns, and once you pass a certain sample size, doing more interviews makes little sense, unless you need that larger sample to break out key subgroups, such as by age, gender, income, etc. For this reason, and also because it sounds like a lot of people, most national polls use a sample of 900-1000 people, because the average accuracy, or sampling error, with that sample size is about three percentage points. Doubling the sample to 2000 only increases the accuracy by one point to about two points. So it is not cost efficient to have larger samples when the same conclusions would be made anyway.

It is not true that if you are surveying in, or projecting to, a larger area, such as the total U.S. versus only Iowa, that you need a larger sample. Perhaps strange as it may seem, the size of the population (for example, the U.S. or Iowa) has no relationship to the size of the sample needed to project the sample to the population. If you need 900 interviews nationally to come within three percentage points of accuracy, you also need 900 interviews in Iowa to come within three percentage points. Now, of course, if you wanted to be as accurate in Iowa and in every other state as you are nationally, then you would need 900 interviews in every state, or 45,000 in total. But no one wants to be that accurate. If you are in Iowa, you are probably surveyed in Iowa and want the accuracy for Iowa. If you are doing a national poll, you still want the three-point accuracy, but you don't want it in every state. (Unless you are the federal government, and sometimes they actually do want that level of accuracy, but then it is our tax dollars they are spending on the poll, not their own dollars.)

Aside from the statistical answer to sampling and population ratios, you can imagine how difficult if

would be if the size of the sample DID depended upon
the size of the population. You would need a formula
showing every possible population size from 30 to 200
million, with a different sample size for each. "Let's see,
for a survey in Greenville SC, I need 201 respondents;
for South Carolina I need 457, for the Southeast 620,
and for the total U.S, I need 907. But wait, I am only
interested in Greenvillians who are between 21 and 49
years of age who drink beer. How do I know how many
there are in the population until I do the survey, but I
can't do the survey until I decide how many to interview." Fortunately, the god of sampling error has taken
that into account and simply decreed once you know the
sample size, you can project the error, not the other way
around.

The typical adult, who doesn't have all these neat
facts that researchers know about sample size and sampling error and who doesn't see how a sample of 900
can represent 100 million, often is called to sit on a
jury where a survey may be introduced. The side who
is trying to critique a survey will often use this lack of

information to convince a jury that the sample is too small and should be given no weight in evidence.

In Deland, Florida, a local gasoline distributor tried to get a survey by a particular gas station chain thrown out of court because the national chain had done a survey with "only" 600 customers. The questioning process went something like this:

> Plaintiff's lawyer: (to the researcher who did the survey for the defendant), "Do you know how many customers your client has in this gas station each month?"
>
> Defendant (the researcher): "No."
>
> Plaintiff: "Would it surprise you to learn that the gas station has over 16,000 customers per month?"
>
> Defendant: "No."

(But let's interject at this point that the researcher knew the next question would be something like:

Plaintiff: "How can you say that your survey of 600 customers is representative of over 16,000 customers?"

Defendant: "You are going to ask me if surveying 600 people can represent 16,000. Let me tell you why it can. Assume you are cooking soup on a stove and you have a quart saucepan on the front burner with a pint of soup. And you also have a ten gallon pan of soup on the back burner. You want to taste the soup to see if it tastes right. That is, you want to "sample" the soup. So you take a tablespoon to taste the soup in the quart saucepan and also the same tablespoon to taste the soup in the larger container. You don't need to use a tablespoon for the quart saucepan and then drink an entire cup from the larger container. You use the same spoon—the same sample size—regardless of the size of the soup.")

This answer always works. Even if the opposing attorney thinks quickly enough (and they never do) to ask if you would get all the peas and vegetables from the large saucepan with only a teaspoon. The answer to this is that if you want to taste all segments of soup, and assuming the vegetables are evenly distributed—a random sample of soup and its ingredients—the answer is that you would need a larger sample for **both** containers.

5.

Sampling error is either one of the last things you should be concerned about–or one of the most important.

When seeing a press report about a survey, especially those "national polls" always too briefly summarized in the media, the most common feature is a small note at the bottom of each chart or table or a sentence to this effect: "The sampling error in this survey is plus or minus 3.2%." This is intended to make the reader confident in the findings from the research: even though there are over 200 million people in this country, the survey is so accurate that the true answer is only 3.2% away. Missing from this statement are some important other comments, which of course have too much detail to go into in the paper or a five second TV screen shot.

The first thing missing in this statement of sampling error is that it assumes we have a perfectly random survey: in this case, of every adult person in the country or in the identified survey area, or if it is a poll of voters, a totally random sample of all voters in the area. Rarely is this true, however. Most of the time it is, of course, a telephone poll of people who were at home at the time of the phone call, who can speak the language of the interviewer, who agree to be surveyed in the first place, who could understand presumably neutral or unbiased survey questions, who were truthful to the interviewer, and whose answers were properly recorded, correctly entered into the computer, and were properly analyzed. Researchers know the extent to which all of these things are true, or not, of course, but you won't often find it in the report of the poll's findings.

What is usually also missing is a statement that this is the **average** sampling error, not the error for every percentage answer, and certainly not for subgroups such as men versus women, or younger versus older voters. If we look at findings for men versus women, and there are 500 of each in the total sample of 1000, the sampling error of $+-$ three points for a sample of 1000 becomes $+/-$ four points for a sample of 500. And if we are interviewing people who make up, say, 12% of the population, or 120 people, the error on that cell is actually plus/minus ten percentage points, meaning that if 50 % answer "yes" to a question, the true answer is between 40% and 60%, or a 20 point range.

The reader should note that the sample of 500 had a four point sampling error and a doubling of the sample to 1000 only reduced the error to three points, which perfectly illustrates the difference in the small reduction in error compared to the large increase in sample size.

But the actual sampling error to a given question also depends upon the specific percentage answer and is not always (and in most cases it is not) that 3.2%. If there are 1000 people in the survey, and the (average) sampling error is reported as $+/-$ 3.2 percent, it means that this is the average sampling error or the error if the percentage answer to a given question is between 40-60% (i.e., 45% say they will vote for a certain candidate). If a smaller or larger proportion, such as 20% or 95%, gave a certain answer, the sampling error is different: it might be plus/minus 2%, or plus/minus 4%, depending upon the answer. However, that's too complicated to explain in a table, so the easy way out is to just use one sampling error number.

Rarely, too, is it explained that this sampling error is at the "95% confidence level." This means that if we did the survey the same way 100 times, 95 times out of those 100, the findings could be projected within those three percentage points. So, if, for example, our study showed 55% favoring a particular candidate, we know the true percentage—if we had asked everyone—would be no more than 58% ($55 + 3$) or any less than 52% ($55 - 3$).

But we don't have to be "95% confident." We might choose a higher confidence level to be more accurate.

After all, if you drive to work everyday being 95% confident you won't have an accident at any intersection, you would probably have an accident every day if on a given trip to the office you go 95 blocks or once you made 100 trips. Or suppose you've taken 95 plane trips in the past few years without an accident. Often even 99.9% accuracy is not high enough. But for survey research, it's too expensive to do enough interviews to be any more accurate than 95%, and in any case it is "close enough for government work."

On the other hand, sometimes a lower accuracy level is sufficient. In a political poll, you might be satisfied with 90% accuracy: 90 times out of 100, the findings would be within that same sampling error. Or you could be even less accurate. We recently saw a study which had such a small sample size that the report said the findings were accurate plus or minus 40 points. This means that if a specific answer was at 50%, then the true value in the population would be 50 +/− 40 points, or between 10-90%! I think that if that is the degree of your accuracy, you might as well guess.

But most of the time you don't have to worry about all this. Why? Because most published polls always have a large enough sample to be accurate enough to reasonably project a number close to the reported number. So, just read the numbers as they are reported and don't even think about sampling error, because if the writers are doing their job, they should mention when the numbers are "too close to call."

Why is the sampling error often reported with a decimal point? Because it is more accurate? Not at all. It's because the use of a percentage decimal point (notice the sampling error note said plus/minus 3.2%, not simply 3%) is used to **pretend** that the study is more accurate than it really is. Does anyone draw a different conclusion if the finding were 58.3% instead of 58%? Of course not. But 58.3% sounds more accurate. Just as though if it is 21 degrees outside, it is for all intents and purposes as cold as if it were 20 degrees or 22 degrees. You don't put on a heavy coat at 21 degrees or remove it at 22. Not rounding percentages, reporting them to a decimal point, is spurious accuracy. Sounds good but doesn't really mean anything.

So much for sampling error when you as a typical citizen are reading published polls. You can safely ignore the sampling error. (It's virtually always plus/minus three points anyway, and you don't have the error for sub-samples in any case.) But if you are writing research reports or are in the business of reading and acting upon research reports for your company, then you do need to pay attention to sampling error.

Sometimes that's difficult to do, however, because so many reports either clutter up the tables with all kinds of footnotes and nomenclature, or they don't mention it at all. More importantly, if the only decisions which are made from a research report are those where the answers exceed sampling error, then most decisions would not be made, because the sample sizes are not enough, statistically, to be 95% confident. Instead, the reader is wise to look at directional differences, as well as to take a lower level of confidence.

Seasoned researchers have found that much of the time, the lack of statistical significance is only because the sample sizes are too small for the standard cut-off points to be 95% confident. In other words, it is not random fluctuation in the data, but rather that if you had a larger sample, the findings would be significant. Let's not decline to form an opinion simply because we had a few less people.

Look at these awareness levels for two brands for two successive years. Based on the sample size, the first brand is statistically different from year to year, but the second brand is not. Yet who would deny that in reality, the awareness of both brands has more than likely increased.

Claimed Brand Awareness Trends

	2000	2001
	(400)	(400)
Brand A	35%	49%
Brand B	42%	48%

Before we begin to pin too much importance to sampling error, however, we need to look at the underpinnings of sampling error, which brings us to the next secret in marketing research.

6.

Marketing research is based on the theory of random sampling, yet there is no such thing as a random sample (unless you are a coin).

Although marketing research has mushroomed in the last fifty years, the concept of random sampling goes back much further than that and has been the one cornerstone of marketing research. The theory, which is totally accurate, well-tested, and proven, says that to test a theory, event, or hypothesis, you don't need to question or examine the **entire** population, rather you can draw a **sample** and project from that sample.

Sampling is an old concept and arose before marketing research itself did. As early as 1279 A.D., King Edward I of England had his mint sample the gold and silver coins they produced to determine if the coins had the proper gold or silver content. It was not necessary to test every coin, just a sample. (How they determined which coins to sample, if they used a random sample, have been lost in history.)

When the concept of sampling is introduced in textbooks, or in lay literature, the most-used example is that of tossing a coin. You have a penny and toss it 100 times. About half (and the "about" qualifier is important) of those times it will come up heads and about half it will come up tails. You can toss it 100, 500, or 1000 times or more, and it will always come up about 50/50. But two things happen. First, as you begin tossing it several hundred times, the percentage of heads/tails will stay bout 50/50. Tossing it 500 times will show about 50/50, as will tossing it 10,000 times. In other words, you don't need to toss it that long, rather you can take a sample, say a sample of 100 tosses, and still get about 50/50.

Very true. When you toss a coin, the coin has two sides, and it always has to be either heads or tails (unless you drop it in a crack). You have full knowledge of the possible answers and know that except for production difference, a penny here is a penny there. And you only project to "all pennies." That all pennies are alike is taken for granted.

But pennies are not dimes or questions, and people are not coins. If you interview (a sample of) people in a mall, you are interviewing only a sample of those people who are in the mall at that time and will talk to you. Some people never go to a mall. People with different characteristics go to different malls than other people, and some go at different times than others. Many people won't talk to you, so you don't know who they are or what their opinions are. (Who ever heard of a coin refusing to be tossed or refusing to land on either heads or tails?)

The point is, you never have a true random sample of adults. You don't even have a random sample of people in the mall (very likely because mall interviews tend to be done mainly during high traffic times so that the cost of the interview is less). The most you have, if that, and if the study is properly done over different day-parts and days, is a **sample of people who are in the mall at that time and who will talk with you.** These people may (or may not) be very different from people who buy your brand.

Now, mall interviewing is a very accepted form of interviewing. In fact, it is essentially the only way much research is or can be done, given the demise of door-to-door sampling. Under door-to-door sampling, the researcher obtains a list of all residential dwelling units in a given area and uses a random starting point and a random interval between houses (e. g, every 5th house). Interviewers go out and knock on doors. If no one answers, they are supposed to return at a later time.

But no one does this any more unless you are the U.S. Census and have several billion dollars to spend. And even then the purported "census" is not really a

census, it's just households you knew existed and those
you could reach and those who would co-operate with
you. In fact, it is likely that a good sample is more purported than a properly conducted census.

Today, many people will not open their door to
strangers. We actually know of a study where the interviewer killed the respondent, although the details of this
event some 15 or 20 years ago is unclear. We heard it
went something like this:

Interviewer on the phone to supervisor: "I was
not able to get the last interview."

Supervisor: "Why not?"

Interviewer: "I killed the respondent."

What the supervisor said next is unknown.

Even if technically a random sample plan could be
designed, the concept of random door-to-door sampling
breaks down in practice. If there is a large fence around
the house and an angry German shepherd in the yard,

do you think the hourly interviewer is going inside the fence? Rather, she (most interviewers are female) will probably write down either "not home" or "vacant unit" and go on to the next house.

But I digress from mall interviewing. The point is that there are millions of mall intercepts done very year with perfectly useful results. And researchers continue to use "sampling error" in their reports of mall intercepts, even though no mall intercept is a true random sample.

For the reader who may interested, mall intercepts use "quota samples" instead of "random samples." Because researchers know that mall shopper demographics vary by which mall they are in, and that malls have more female than male shoppers, quotas are assigned: "We want 50 adults between the ages of 21 and 65, half of whom are female and half are male, and of the total 50, 35 must be heavy users of laundry detergents, with 50% of users saying their usual brand is Tide."

But I have never seen a report on a mall intercept study where in the Preface or Limitations, there was a statement such as: **this study only reflects the opinions of people in selected malls who walked by an interviewer in certain malls during certain hours and allowed themselves to be surveyed, and thus respondents' opinions may not really represent all the users of Brand X.** Yet, there is always a table of sampling error.

7.

One of the most popular marketing research tools– the focus group–is the most dangerous one.

No one is sure when the first focus group was conducted. After all, the term focus group is simply another name for a discussion session, typically with 8-12 people, in which the topic is "focused" in given areas, but it may be the single most popular marketing research technique. There are over 1000 focus group facilities in the U.S., and over 200,000 such focus groups are conducted annually. Just about everybody does focus groups. (That's one of the problems, of course: they are too easy to do.)

Focus groups are often used for several reasons, some of which are invalid ones. True, focus groups are fast (they can be set up in a few days to a week), inexpensive compared to quantitative research, and can provide some basic and sometimes in-depth learning within the "fast and inexpensive" (some would say "quick and dirty") context.

To elaborate, focus groups can be helpful if properly used, and there are many valid reasons for conducting them:

To learn consumer language and terminology.

To test assumptions or hypotheses regarding reactions to proposed new products and services.

To demonstrate to clients not familiar with the technique how little consumers may know or care about the new concept. But even then focus groups have limitations and can be abused. They are directional, not projectable; indicative not quantitative. And you don't make groups projectable by doing **more** focus groups, although some practitioners believe that.

Pity the poor moderator whose client wanted to do sixteen focus groups: (two in each of eight cities) because their competition was different in each city. Any moderator in this situation would soon find herself (most moderators are female, which is an interesting topic in itself) asking the group participants in the third or fourth city: "Pardon me, but have I asked you this before?"

The truth is that while the competitive environment may well differ by city, in virtually all product and service categories, the attitudes that drive decisions and how people think about products and brands do not. Further, differences of this type, if they do exist, are rightfully found in quantitative studies. After all, imagine how many telephone interviews could be conducted for the price of sixteen focus groups.

Focus groups rely, and sometimes rely too much, on what people verbalize in a group. When people start talking, either with strangers or friends, they never want to put themselves in a bad light or reflect unfavorably on themselves. So they often say things that sound good: "I'm not influenced by advertising" is a perfect example. Well, if that were true, there would never be any advertising. But we know advertising influences people, regardless of what they say.

Focus group moderators (a moderator is called a "facilitator" in all disciplines other than marketing research) must constantly be on guard to prevent a focus group participant who may have a dominating personality, or may quickly be seen to have more knowledge than the other participants, from leading the discussion. Sometimes the moderator must remove a particular person from the room because his or her influence is so high.

We once had to remove a lawyer from a group because he got off on a tangent saying that to even discuss real estate developments in a focus group on behalf of a residential development client meant the client was violating the law by having the focus group since the group discussion was not preceded by a prospectus.

In a different situation, one of the clients wanted to sit in the group, "as a participant," in order to get the discussion going in the direction desired. The problem was, that any time a participant made a negative comment about her company's product, she felt obligated to defend it. The group was ruined.

Clients, like individual participants, are often influenced by their previous experience in focus groups. If someone has had a bad focus group experience (easy enough to have), he may well be biased against such groups. If that same client has done focus groups and the group participants really liked his new product idea, then he more than likely is a big fan of focus groups because they told him what he wanted to hear. This is one of the real problems in groups: the tendency to interpret conversations from group members in light of the observer's own experience.

Another problem is that the findings are often taken literally. Just because one or two people, or an entire group of people say something in a group does not mean you should take their advice. A typical viewer comment would be, "I know I'm only one person, but…"

A few years ago a state regulatory authority on apples would not allow their state's apple growers to sell apples with less than a two inch diameter because they said focus groups told them that apples smaller than two inches were inferior apples. Such nonsense. Millions of dollars in wasted apples that had to be fed to hogs just because a couple of people in a focus group made such an offhand comment.

You should cringe—and rightly so—when you read, and I read this often, that proposed advertising was "tested" in focus groups and found to be either great or terrible advertising. Commercials should never be "tested" in focus groups, because a focus group is not a test. A focus group can provide direction to advertising, but to rely upon what a group of people say about advertising in a group where it is cool to say you are not influenced by advertising, is foolish.

In doing a focus group on breath mints, one lady was adamant about why she used Certs breath mints. "It's certainly not because of the advertising," she said, very determinedly. It is because (and she holds up her arms and touches the forefinger of each hand together) "it's two mints in one."

Never, never, never test commercials in focus groups. Show them if you will for one reason or another, but never refer to this, or use this, as any test of advertising.

Beware of any report on a focus group that reports numbers: three participants said this, two said that. If someone in a ten-member group makes a comment, this cannot be projected to 10% of the population, but rather only that that is an attitude which exists. Again, focus groups are not projectable. But they are great tools of learning, especially to clients who only hear from their friends, spouses, neighbors or relatives about how great their products or services are. Just knowing how little information most people have on certain products, what they don't know and what they do not care to know, is extremely important.

Also, beware of any focus group report that reports mean ratings: Attribute A got a mean rating of 5.4, Attribute B a rating of 6.7. There is no statistical validity to the reliability of such meaningless scores, and you should run away from any report that has them.

And beware of wanting to do focus groups because they are "cheap." Conducting focus groups because they cost less than other techniques is using the wrong decision criteria. They may cost less in dollars than other techniques, but the true cost may well be in the cost of incorrect, misleading, or wrong information.

8.

The way most mean ratings are used, they may be meaningless.

A common reporting technique to evaluate brands is a "mean rating," which is simply the average rating on a scale, such as an average of 7.4 on a ten-point scale. The higher the number, the more positive the rating, though some researchers make it difficult by reversing the scales so that the lower the number the better. (Anyone who has ever tried to explain this will never reverse the ratings in their next report.)

"Mean" rating is an interesting term beyond its technical definition. Actually, the ratings aren't mean at all, but you ought to get mad at how some people use them.

What would you do with a table like this where four brands are rated on four attributes on a 1 to 10 scale?

	Brand A	Brand B	Brand C	Brand D
Overall	8.10	7.87	7.81	8.04
Quality	8.11	7.98	7.45	7.47
Convenience	8.21	7.99	8.10	8.25
Value	8.32	8.01	8.24	7.99

In a table like this, the researcher has not done her job. She's merely typed up numbers on a word processor and left the reader to figure out what it means. The job of a market researcher is not only to retype numbers, but most importantly, to draw summaries, conclusions, and recommendations from the numbers.

Means can be misinterpreted because the mean rating does not tell you anything about how the ratings are distributed. It can also be misleading when used in place of other measures of averages, such as **mode** and **median.**

For clarification, "mean rating" is simply the nomenclature used for one of three different ways to calculate an average. Other measures are "mode," which is the most common answer, and the "median," which is the point at which half the people are above and half the people are below. Sometimes the differences are important, since a mean is highly influenced by two extremes: those that are either very high or very low. In this example, all three measures of average household income could be correct:

Mean income $75,000 (total income divided by number of households)

Median income $56,000 (half the households earn more than this, half earn less)

Mode $45,000 (the most common amount in the survey)

Already you see the opportunity for selective reporting. If you are trying to show your product appeals to people of high income, use the mean. If you want to show that it appeals to the typical household, use the median or mode. All are correct because each is defined in a different matter.

But you don't always know which definition is used. If an "average" age or average income is reported, without the proper definition of mean, median, or mode, any of the three could be used.

Definitions are fairly easy to master. But interpretation of mean ratings for brands or products or concepts is more difficult. Suppose you test two products and find the following mean ratings on "overall quality:"

Mean Product Ratings

	Product A	3.00
	Product B	3.00

Given this information, and this information alone, you would conclude that Product A is equal to Product B. And if Product B is the new formula and cheaper to produce than A, you might be tempted to recommend going to formula B. But wait, there's more!

Let's look at the distribution of these ratings:

Distribution of Product Ratings

	Product A	Product B
	(#)	(#)
Rated Excellent	10	25
Rated Good	10	—
Rated Average	10	—
Rated Fair	10	—
Rated Poor	10	25
Total	50	50
Mean	3.00	3.00

Of course, you could also calculate a median or mode for the above, but nobody would do that, would they?

Now, the conclusions and especially the recommendation are not so easy. Product A has a wide degree of appeal, whereas Product B is polarized. Half the sample loves it, and half hates it. Yet, both products have the same overall rating. So you have to look at more than means, you also have to look at the distribution of ratings, such as % top box, % total positive, and % total negative.

But wait, there's still more.

Some people are more discriminating or able to tell the difference more than others. For example, some people might rate two products the same on every attribute, and others might show a wide range. If these people are distributed evenly across the population, then it does not matter. However, it is more than likely that certain kinds of people (young, old, heavy users, etc.) rate products differently than their counterparts, and the overall averages will mask that. Some people are always more critical. So a 4.00 rating for one person may not mean the same thing as a 4.00 rating for another person.

Still another situation is that some brands (obviously) have higher shares than others. This affects the ratings. Let's say we ask consumers to rate McDonald's hamburgers and Judy's burgers. McDonald's will get a higher rating than Judy's, even if we screen for users of each, because there will be more people in the sample who have tried McDonald's. So even if we screen for users, there will be more people whose usual brand is McDonald's than whose usual brand is Judy's, and since people who claim a usual brand normally rate it higher than other brands, McDonald's will show higher ratings than Judy's. Yet Judy's may be the better product.

Some people call this the "double jeopardy" effect. A low selling brand is penalized twice: first for being low selling, and second, because it is low selling, it also receives lower ratings. The marketing significance of this is that you can't raise the brand ratings by doing anything about the brand attributes; you can only increase the brand ratings by increasing the sales of the product.

The former president of Chrysler Corporation, Robert Lutz, in his book *Guts*, has an entire chapter on mean ratings and their mis-use. He points out that if the average rating of a new proposed car is, say, 5.00 out of 10, it means the car is "average." But what if half of those respondents rated it a 9 or 10 and the other half rated it a 0 or 1? Such a finding would show that there might well be a market to a small portion of the population who really liked it. This, in fact, was the situation of the then-new Dodge Ram pickup truck: 80% of truck owners disliked it, but the 20% who loved it, really loved it, and went out in droves and bought it.

Just because you have mean ratings does not mean you need to use them as such, when there may be better ways to show the same information. One way is multiply the mean rating by ten, converting a 7.2 rating to 72%. This indicates that that brand is rated 72% of its maximum possible rating, a concept which is often easier for non-researchers to understand than 7.2 or 7.23. If you have a five-point scale and the mean is 3.2, then this is 64% of the maximum possible rating.

Still another way is to look at "top box," or "top 2 boxes," or "top 3 boxes" of the mean. For example, instead of a mean rating of 3.2 on a 5 point scale or a 64%, look at the percentage of respondents who rated in the highest possible (i.e., top box) rating, or the percentage who rated it top 2 boxes, or "Excellent/Good." Going further, you could look at the extent to which the top two boxes (positive) exceeded the bottom two (negative).

When dealing with a simple 5 point Excellent to Poor scale, top box and top two boxes are very easy to understand. It's helpful to know how many people rate your product "excellent," and how many rate it "excellent or good."

The "top box" concept does not work as well with scales of more than five points, such as a seven-point scale or a ten-point scale. If you have a seven-point scale (which we do not recommend, but which is commonly used) and you find, for example, that 44% rate the brand a 6 or a 7, it's hard to do much with that.

If you use a ten-point scale, from 1 to 10, then you are faced with what levels to show. Do you show top box 10 (very difficult to achieve since many people won't rate a brand 10 out of 10), do you show top 2 boxes (the percentage giving a 9 or a 10), or do you look at top 3 box, which is the percentage rating a 8, 9, or 10? The lower you go, the higher you can make the numbers. So, do you want high or low ratings?

Let's talk about how many points a scale should have, in the next chapter.

9.

It doesn't make any difference what kind of rating scales you use: ten point, seven point, or five point scales are all the same.

Now of course this does not mean they all produce the same ratings, but rather than they will produce the same conclusions: as long as you are consistent and use the same scales each time. Don't change from a 5-point scale on Wave I to a 10-point scale on Wave II because you won't be able to compare the findings. And don't even start to think that you can convert a 5-point scale to a 10-point scale by doubling a five point or halving the

10-point. That does not work. Actually, to convert from a five point scale to a ten point scale, you double the five point scale rating and then subtract one. But that's another story.

Most people are familiar with five point scales, such as Excellent-Good-Average-Fair-Poor or some such wording, or a ten point scale, which usually just asks you to rate a product on a 1 to 10 scale with the higher the number the more positive you are. But that's only scratching the surface.

How many different scales can you name? The 1992 American Marketing Association's *Marketing Scale Handbook*—not the only book written on scaling but probably the most expensive one on the price scale (published at $149.95, cheaper in a paperback version)—actually shows 588 different scales. And it discusses each one in depth. One page per scale.

One of most interesting scales—not in the book—is an open-end scale, also called an unanchored scale. It's very simple to administer: "Please rate this product using any number you want, depending upon how much you like or dislike it. You can rate it 10 million, or minus 50 or any number you want."

The problem, however, comes when you want to process the ratings. If you use the arithmetic mean, very high or very low numbers cause a large skew. If one person rates a product 1 million, and 20 rate it 10, the mean rating will be 47,628. And that hardly helps if you only know the mean. If you use a median, then the rating of 1 million might just as easily been 50,000 because the median won't change. And if you use the mode, the mode would be 20, the most common answer. So while the concept of "rate it anything you want" sounds great, it is totally impractical in general use.

In analyzing scale data using the mean or arithmetic average, most people are prone to make their findings sound more precise than they really are, without realizing it. This is a mistake most people make: the computer calculates the mean as 7.23, and so you report 7.23.

But what does 7.23 really mean (no pun intended) versus, for example, a 7.19?

All scale ratings should be rounded. Not 7.23, or 7.19, but 7.2 and 7.2. There is no marketing or statistical difference between a scale rounded to two decimal places and a scale rounded only to one decimal place; it's just that the one with two decimal points sounds more accurate. Another way is to multiply by 10; so rather than 7.2 persons, there is 72% of the maximum positive. This is easier to explain than 7.23. We know one company who requests that all percentage answers, even those on a sample as small as 600, be rounded to two decimal places. In reality, even one decimal place is too much. Who cares if 55.67% feel one way instead of 56% who feel that way?

And one time we had a request to reverse the standard rounding rule, used by most people, that says when rounding from a decimal point of .5, you round to an even. Thus, 69.5 rounds to 70; 70.5 rounds to 70. The theory is, that over all the data, doing it half one-way and half the other will "even out," especially when adding percentages in a table. This client wanted us to rewrite the entire report and "round to odd." Thus, 69.5 rounds to 69; 70.5 rounds to 71. We did it, of course, but it seemed that more time should have been spent on what the data meant, rather than how to re-round the seventeen percentages that in the computer printout ended with .5.

Just like any other statistic, mathematical formulas are used to show whether or not a rating of 7.2 is statistically different from 7.0. And it may be, but so what? What different conclusion are you going to draw from 7.0 versus 7.2?

But you really can't apply statistical error theory to scalar data, without a big limitation you will never see anywhere. If you asked a good statistician about statistical differences in scale ratings, that statistician would tell you that you really can't apply such theory to scales, because what is a 4 rating to some people is a 6 to another. And if one person's 4 is the same as another's 6, then you can't really count them the same way. But people do it anyway, because what else can you do?

To illustrate: Say a person is rating a brand on six attributes, and her ratings are 4,4,4,4,4 and 5. Clearly to that individual, a 5 rating is different from a four, otherwise she would have given a 4 rating to the 5 attribute. But when averaged across the total sample, even if dozens of people reacted the same, it would not make any "statistical" difference, meaning that the 5 rating of the person who rated everything else a 4 would be considered the same rating.

Have you ever noticed that virtually all scales of less than two digits never use an even number of scale points? There are few four point, six point, or eight point scales, because these even number scales do not allow for a "no opinion" response. If you feel the product is average, and the scale is Excellent-Good-Fair-Poor, what number do you give it?

Some researchers purposely use four point or six point scales, however, because they want to force someone to give an opinion. But we all know, or should know, that if people who have no opinion on a topic are

"forced" to give an opinion, their opinions will ultimately divide the same way of those who had an opinion. To illustrate; if we have voting preferences of 60%
candidate A, and 30% candidate B, with 10% who cannot state preference, you can either force those 10% to
give an opinion or simply re-percentage the 60 and 30
to 90, resulting in an overall preference of 67%.
Ignoring them is the same as splitting them proportion-
ately. However, this also assumes that those 10% (or the
60% and the 30% for that matter) will go to the polls and
vote, but that is another issue.

10.

You can't measure the effectiveness of advertising by asking people if it effective.

(Corollary: You can't measure the effectiveness of advertising by asking people if they like the advertising.)

These errors abound. How many times have you seen a table showing the percentage of customers who responded "advertising" when asked what caused them to buy the brand? In truth, stated proportions of consumers who say advertising causes them to purchase are almost always understated. And there are many reasons for that. First, many people do not know it was advertising that created their positive attitudes preceding purchase. Secondly, they may not want to admit it. Thirdly, advertising is often a link, sometimes the first link, in building awareness, interest, attitudes, intent, and purchase.

Take the tourism industry, for example. A Georgia resident sees an ad for Louisiana and calls the toll-free number to request a brochure. The brochure comes in the mail and as a result, a trip to Louisiana is made. Yet, if this visitor were asked what caused her to visit Louisiana, she would most likely say the travel brochure, either forgetting or not knowing it was the magazine advertising that caused her to ask for the brochure in the first place.

Whether in focus groups or if questioned alone, many consumers express an intense dislike for utility advertising, because in their opinion it is a monopoly and why does a monopoly need to advertise? Also, since advertising costs money, they believe that if there was no advertising, their energy bills would be lower. Why not cut out advertising and reduce the bills?

In one focus group, one lady was particularly incensed. "It is a big monopoly, and there is no reason to advertise." Twenty minutes later, when the group was discussing ways to conserve energy, this same lady went on and on about how she had learned to turn down her thermostat, put in better insulation and weather stripping, and so on. When asked where she learned all this, she said she saw an ad on TV for the power company! Yet to her, that was not advertising, but rather useful information brought to her by the power company.

Effective advertising does many things, all of which can be measured: An effective ad or ad campaign has one or more of these objectives:

— It makes people aware of the brand.
— It produces brand salience.
— It generates favorable attitudes or imagery towards the brand.
— It increases interest in buying or using the product or service.

And whether not the respondent recalls the advertising (as long as we know they were exposed to it) or likes it does not matter, regardless of what *USA Today* or other Likeability polls say.

11.

Understanding how people respond or do not respond to questions is one mark of a good researcher.

What are some of the problems in questionnaire design?

A. Most people don't make the subtle differences that researchers often make.

Back in South Carolina in the mid 1960's, a leading national research firm was commissioned to find out if the voting public would support liberalizing the liquor laws in the state on behalf of the tourist industry, which suffered in tourist areas because of restrictive liquor regulations. (It still

does, by the way.) Although South Carolina was a classic
"bible belt state" and although its residents probably
thought their friends, neighbors and relatives should not
drink, would it nevertheless be alright for **hotels** to sell
liquor, because then only the tourists would drink so that the
state would have more tax revenue? As part of the extensive
door-to-door statewide survey (back when door to door surveys were done), the researchers asked among others questions, these two: the first one to show, as expected, that local
residents should not drink, and the second to show that it
would be OK for tourists to drink. The two questions:

> *" Are you in favor or opposed to liquor by the drink
> being sold in bars, restaurants, hotels, and lounges
> in South Carolina?"*

> *Are you in favor or opposed to liquor by the drink
> being sold only in **hotel** restaurants and lounges in
> South Carolina?"*

So what happened? The residents of South Carolina
answered both questions exactly the same way. Liquor by
the drink should not be sold in **any** place in South Carolina,
and it should not be sold in hotel restaurants and lounges.

Many respondents did not listen carefully to the slight or subtle difference between the two questions and felt they were the same question. But perhaps more importantly, they held to their beliefs: if it is wrong to have liquor by the drink in any place, it is also wrong to have it (only) in hotels.

If it is wrong, it is wrong. You can't get away with selling an evil product (said the respondents) just by selling it only at some places and not others. (And if the New York research firm, which did the study, had ever spent any time in South Carolina, or had pre-tested the questionnaire, they would have known that from the very beginning.)

B. Most consumers don't really have much interest in survey research topics.

For all the details in wording questions about what clients feel are important topics (and they **are** important to them), most consumers don't really care. And because they don't really care, they often do not listen carefully enough to the questions, nor do they have the interest to take the time. One answer can be as good as another.

Now, certainly there are many product categories where consumers do care a great deal: those where a great deal of money is involved, for example, a house; those who are avid fans of a given activity, such as collector car owners or stereo buffs. But the vast majority of surveys and polls are on more mundane issues: supermarket shopping, banking, long distance phone service, household cleaning products, and on and on.

As researchers, we can't do much to increase survey participants' interest in different products and services. But we can, and should, do a great deal in making the survey interesting, and there are many ways to do this: shorter questionnaires, easier to understand questionnaires, and questionnaires that understand the styles of the consumers we are surveying, questionaires that use the proper language and terminology.

Some researchers may want to ask the same question two different ways to be sure the respondent is consistent, or by inserting "trick" questions, or by sometimes reversing rating scales presumably to cause the consumer to think more carefully about an issue. But you should only ask a question one way, the right way. If you ask a question two different ways and get the same answer, then you have wasted everyone's time. If you ask the question two different ways and get two different answers, then how do you know which one is right?

C. Survey respondents often say things they think the interviewer wants to hear.

If a survey is conducted so openly that the respondent knows, or can guess the sponsor, the respondent will tend to give positive, pleasing answers. Generally speaking, consumers do not want confrontations. If you are a fast food restaurant customer and are being questioned in the restaurant, you will not likely tell the interviewer or a restaurant employee that the food is bad, or the service is lousy, or that the prices are too high. Have you even been in a restaurant where, perhaps, your steak was not cooked properly enough, and the server comes by and says, "How is your meal?" It is the rare customer who says "terrible," or "you are unfriendly," or "I am never coming back." Rather, you just smile and say "fine." And then you don't go back.

D. Even minute changes in question wording and phrasing can make a difference in the answers.

By careful question phrasing, answers can be predicted. Want to get high customer satisfaction? Ask the positive response first: "How does your current new car compare to others you have had: it is better, about the same, or not as good?" To generate more negative responses, ask it this way: "How does your current new car compare to others you have had: it is worse, about the same, or better?"

Want to lead to a yes answer? Ask: "Do you agree that this product is a great value?"

Want to lower the yes answers? Ask: "Do you agree that this product is a good value or a poor value?"

Do you need to show a high preference in a taste test? Ask, "Which of the products do you prefer?" Or if you want a lower preference, ask: "Which of the products do you prefer, **or does it not make any difference to you?**"

E. Consumers are often mis-informed, and they answer on this mis-information.

If you ask consumers how much of each dollar of their average power bill goes as profit to the power company, you might hear answers as high as 50 cents. Yet, the true answer is about 5 cents. Now, of course learning about this mis-information may well be the purpose of the research and that is what you have to deal with.

F. People have poor memories.

No criticism is intended, but it is a fact that because of all the routine things we do everyday, and especially how often we do them, it is difficult if not impossible to accurately remember some of the types of things surveyors often ask you to remember, such as (a) how many times

did you go out to eat at a fast food restaurant last month
(b) how many of those times were for breakfast, lunch,
dinner, or a snack (c) and how do you rate the last restaurant you went to on some 17 different attributes? So, ask
a question, get an answer, even if it is the wrong answer,
or an answer inaccurately remembered. Don't remember
(or don't want to admit) that the last brand of bacon you
ate was an inexpensive private label brand, that's no problem, just say Oscar Mayer, the brand that first comes to
mind. (In surveys on refrigerated packaged meat, the proportion of consumers who give a private label brand is
vastly understated and major brands overstated from actual sales statistics. And this is true for most categories where
private label brands have substantial market shares.)

G. Don't confuse a popularity contest with marketing research.

Many times, answers about best brands and worst
brands are simply a popularity contest, nothing else. Ask
a sample of people who has the best advertising and who
has the worst, the same brands will turn up on both lists.

(This is not true just in questions about advertising. The same fast food restaurant will be chosen as the best restaurant as well as the worst; the same motel chain will be chosen as the best motel chain as well as the worst. The largest bank will have the most satisfied customers as well as the most dissatisfied.)

Now of course it is entirely possible for people to like a given brand's advertising, but it is more than likely that people are just playing back the brands they are most aware of.

For many years the American Marketing Association would show two reels of TV commercials at their annual meeting. One reel would be a reel of commercials, which received awards for advertising effectiveness: increased brand awareness, more favorable attitudes towards the brand, and higher sales. Then they would show a reel of commercials from a TV commercial testing firm, which polled consumers on how much they liked or disliked different commercials. It is not surprising to good researchers that the same commercials were never on both lists, which is another way of saying that just because someone likes a commercial does not mean they will buy the brand.

For many years Lever Brothers ran commercial after commercial for Wisk talking about "ring around the collar." They would get many letters from consumers complaining about this annoying commercial: how long are you going to keep running it?

Eventually, these letters took a toll, and the agency took the commercial off the air (with the client's permission, of course). But then they got **one** letter from the client: put this commercial back on the air because sales were down.

People may hate the commercial, but they may still buy the product. Ask Anacin.

12.

Good research does not have to be expensive. Expensive research is not necessarily good research.

Just as in many products or services, and certainly in marketing research, there is sometimes the feeling that "you get what you pay for." Most people know, or should know, that there are certain brands, especially in the luxury category, where the increase in price outweighs the increase in the quality of the product. But they buy it for a reason, sometimes to make a statement.

And this is true in research. Just because a particular research project costs a great deal more money than another one, does not necessarily mean it is a better piece of research. Yet, because there are no "standard" prices for research, the research buyer has no way to compare quality except by comparing prices of competing providers.

Suppose you are looking at four prices for a study. Ignore for the moment that they may be configured differently or that one might be proposing twice as many interviews as the other:

Provider A	$62,000
Provider B	$65,000
Provider C	$39,800
Provider D	$108,000

What can you tell about these proposals from their pricing? Absolutely nothing. The lower priced study might be just as good as the higher priced one for several reasons. Or it may indicate that that provider totally misunderstands the details of the project. Perhaps the higher priced provider has done this study before and knows the pitfalls. Or maybe that provider just wants to make a higher profit on the job. He does not have to get every job, just a few, and he will make as much money as a company who does twice as much work.

Sometimes companies with an excellent reputation—and there are many of these—charge more because they can. Sometimes lower priced proposals come from a company which needs the work.

The point is, you can't tell. You have to know more than this. Some of the issues to check out include:

* **The firm's research philosophy.** A heady question. But a good research firm will be able to answer this very easily. For example, do they look at research as numbers, or as information? How is research used to make a decision? Are they descriptive or analytical? Do they summarize or interpret?

* **The overall reputation of the firm.** However, it's not unusual for a prospect's knowledge of a research provider to come from sales literature, the company's pitch or presentation, or word of mouth around the

office. When screening potential research providers, check by calling their clients. Realize that most clients will give a positive evaluation, otherwise they would not be on the client list. When talking with clients, ask how the client rates that firm versus other firms they have had experience with. What makes them different? What are the strengths and weaknesses of each firm?

   * **The experience and capabilities of the firm.** There is no research firm which is all things to all people. Some are highly specialized and others highly generalized. Keep in mind, however, that most research techniques transcend specific topic areas. Some industries feel that a research firm needs specific experience in their area, so if you are proposing research in the cable TV or medical industries, for example, it will be hard to get a project unless you have experience there. Sounds like the young college graduate wanting a job: the job requires experience, but he needs the job to get the experience.

   ***What services are being provided.** This is very important. Not just the size and scope of the project, but the design and analytical help provided. Who is really doing the analysis? Sometimes analysis is outsourced. Sometimes focus group moderators, who enjoy conducting the group but hate writing the report, will send the tapes or transcripts to a free-lancer who will write up the report without any real knowledge of the client and client objectives. Beware of this type of reporting.

*Who will actually work on the account? Some research firms have sales people, but the home office does all the work. Are you getting top caliber people on the project? If possible, meet the people and talk with them. You might find that a given supplier is fully capable but the person or persons assigned the account team is not. A good analyst can make the difference between a clear, thoughtful, actionable project and a simple summary of what happened.

*What the project costs. Costs are important, but supplier selection should not be price shopping. Selecting a research provider totally on the basis of price assumes that all suppliers are equal. Some may be more field oriented and others analytically oriented. Some may conduct all the research in-house and others may outsource it. Care should be taken to understand all the elements of the research cost, including charges for additional data runs or analysis after the study is presented.

Section II

The Meaning of Marketing Research

Research tools are all well and good, but once you have mastered the science of research, a good researcher needs to understand the art of research. Numbers and techniques are only a tool to help determine a course of action based on a research project.

The good researcher must know when to use the numbers and when not to use them, such as when the data doesn't make sense relative to what the researcher knows about how people respond and about the market.

13.

The biggest error in marketing research is virtually never mentioned.

Never in the proposal for the study, never in the report, and never in any discussion of the findings. And what is this error?

It's asking the wrong questions (which includes incorrectly wording the right questions), and therefore not finding out what you really wanted to know, but more importantly not even knowing you did not find it out. And going further, it's proceeding to draw the wrong conclusions because you asked the questions the wrong way—and sometimes to the wrong people, but we will get to that later.

The proper wording of the question, if not the most important part of the research project, is at least as important as every other part.

Perhaps the most famous example of asking the question in the wrong way was a study a few years ago, which set out to provide the definitive answer on whether or not people believe the Holocaust really occurred. Findings from this study received a high degree of publicity, because the study seemingly showed that 33% of the American public did not believe the Holocaust actually happened. Is this possible: that one in three think it never happened?

No, that's not possible. What really happened was that the question was phrased in such a misleading and confusing way that many people who felt one way answered in the opposite way. See if you can see which question might give the wrong answer:

Version A. Does it seem possible or does it seem impossible to you that the Nazi extermination of the Jews never happened?

Answer: 33% said it was possible it never happened.

Version B. Do you doubt that the Holocaust actually happened, or not?

Answer: 9% said they doubted it.

As should be clear, Version A used a double negative. Most of those who said "yes it is possible" were actually meaning, "yes, it did happen," but in this case the "yes it's possible" answer really meant no it did not happen. To say that the Holocaust happened required someone to say, "it's impossible it never happened."

But there is still a third way to ask the question to make it even clearer and which shows even a different lower disbelief.

"In your opinion, did the Holocaust definitely happen, probably happen, probably not happen, or definitely not happen?"

Answer: 4% said it probably or definitely did not happen.

One issue under investigation yet asked three different ways, providing three different answers. Take your pick.

All good researchers know that how you ask the question frames the answer. After all, that's how much litigation research is conducted. If you want to prove a certain answer, you ask the question one way. But if you are on the other side, you ask it another way, because you know how the answer will turn out. (And then you just hope you are a better researcher for one side than your researcher friend is for the other side.) That's one reason litigation research is so difficult: you have to design a study for one side that if you were on the other side, you couldn't critique.

It is also important to avoid hinting at the possible answer to the question by how the question is phrased and to avoid leading the respondent to give an answer you want to hear. Sometimes this is done by posing an issue to the respondent, then asking about it.

Here is a real example, which I have disguised slightly:

"If you knew that the biggest threat to the environment is global warming, how much more, per month, in state or local taxes would you be willing to pay to solve this problem?"

Results from this study showed (surprise!) that people wanted to pay more taxes to clean up the environment and that was nice because an environmental group paid for the study. But there are at least five things wrong with this question.

First, it makes a statement that cannot be proven, or at least which many people would disagree with, that global warming is the biggest threat to the environment that presumably must be solved in some fashion.

Second, it attempts to "educate" the respondent, by stating a presumed problem and then following that with only one solution to the problem.

Third, it assumes that people will want to pay more taxes (the question did not ask if they wanted to pay more, it simply said how much more), so it is easier to give an answer rather than say zero.

Fourth, the answer's area is taken at face value. Just because someone says they will pay $11-15 per month in additional taxes does not mean they actually would do so.

Fifth, it assumes that paying more taxes is the way to solve the problem. Just because one might pay $15 more per month does not mean the problem will be solved, and, in fact, there is no promise in the question that it would be solved anyway.

What if the question had been framed differently? Suppose it went something like this:

"Some people say they would be willing to pay as much as $20 per month more in taxes to solve global warming, and others say that there is already enough waste in government spending to solve the problem without a tax increase. Which would you prefer: an additional $20 per month in new taxes, or spending $20 of your taxes more wisely?"

Does anyone doubt what the answer would be to that question? The point is, you can get any answer you want by how you ask the question.

But, of course, as the published survey report on global warming went on to say, the accuracy of the sample was plus/minus 4.5%.

14.

A good researcher can make numbers mean anything he wants them to mean.

I am indebted to Paul Murdoch, a long time friend and advertising agency market researcher, who reports that one day an Account Executive came into his office and saw dozens of computer printouts push-pinned to Paul's office walls.

"Paul," the Account Executive exclaimed: "What do all these numbers mean?"

Paul replies: "They mean anything I want them to mean."

There is perhaps no truer statement of the art of marketing research. Certainly there is science in market research: there is sampling error, regression towards the mean, conjoint, regression, and factor analysis. There are hundreds of software and statistical programs. But it all comes down to the planning, execution, and analysis of marketing research, and that is where the art comes in. It is only in litigation research where art meets science, and where to be relied on in the courtroom, there are rules for marketing research, just as there are rules of evidence.

Paul, by the way, meant that it is up to the researcher to determine what the numbers really mean, and it's not as simple as just looking at the numbers and instantly drawing the conclusions. But others may not be so honest.

I am convinced that most marketing researchers and marketing research departments want to objectively and fairly present unbiased findings. But what do you do when the sponsor of the research purposely changes the meaning of the data by covert actions? Here are two examples:

A very popular insecticide product—now off the market—was originally designed to be used in the kitchen. And that, in fact, was where it was mostly used. However, usage of the product in the kitchen actually violates an EPA regulation because it is not a good idea to place the product in a room where it might contaminate food. What to do in a user survey about where to use the product? Simple. Report the findings like this:

Researchers asked the question: "Where do you use the No Pest Strip?" Researchers were then asked to code each "illegal" use (anyone who said they used it "in the kitchen") as "all other." So here's the table.

Where the No Pest Strip is Used in the Home

72%	All other areas
15%	Bathroom
10%	Outdoor

The manufacturer can now truthfully say that they know of no usage of this product in the kitchen.

Suppose you have a product everyone "knows" causes significant health problems. Similar to the first example above, you ask the research firm to code any answer that this product is dangerous to health, as "all other comments." Here again the manufacturer can claim that they have no knowledge that any consumer has ever said their product is unhealthy or dangerous. This scenario especially happens when they have a blanket rule that in doing focus groups, they can never be taped, and no one other than the interviewer asking the question or the respondent can be in the room. Again, they have no evidence that anyone has ever said their product is dangerous.

Several years ago a magazine publisher printed a portion of a table purporting to show that their magazine beat other publications, and sure enough, their publication was at the top of the list of five publications. Next week, there was a different ad, from a magazine that actually had higher readership, which showed the complete table. The first advertiser had purposely cut off the leading publication from the table. Their claim was that their publication had higher readership than the other four listed. Problem is, there were six magazines in the category.

Well, are there any rules in marketing research? What if a lawyer wrote a paper on how to do marketing research? Well, they have. And it's really a good thing, too.

Here, from the Federal Register in the Manual for Complex Litigation, are the edited "official rules" of marketing research, at least from a litigation standpoint. If every one of these rules were followed and understood in everyday marketing research, we would all be better off:

* The proper universe is identified and examined.

* A representative sample is drawn from that universe.

* The plan for selecting the sample is prepared
  in accordance with generally accepted standards
  of procedure in the field.

* The questionnaire employed in the study is
  prepared in accordance with generally accepted
  standards of procedure, with questions framed
  in a clear, precise, non-leading manner.

* The interviewers are well trained and have
  no knowledge of the anticipated litigation or
  purposes for which the research will be used.

* The interviews are conducted in accordance
  with generally accepted standards of
  procedure in the field.

* The questioning of respondents is correct
  and unbiased.

* Once gathered, the data are accurately analyzed
  and reported.

* The persons designing and conducting the investigation are recognized experts.

The problem is, there are really no rules for marketing research that everybody follows. So we have to have all these secret ones.

And, in fact, the above "rules" raise more questions than they answer, since each point is open to discussion as to what it really means. For example, how do you know if the data are "accurately analyzed and reported?"

Fortunately, a leading research organization, CASRO (Council of American Survey Research Organizations) has stepped in to define these rules. In CASRO's Survey Research Quality Guidelines, CASRO goes into great detail covering problem definition, sample design, interview design, data collection, data processing, and reporting.

All CASRO member firms agree to follow these well-written guidelines and non-members are encouraged to follow them as well.

15.

Marketing significance is more important than statistical significance.

The real value of any survey, poll, or marketing research report is not the statement of the findings, and the associated **statistical** significance, but rather the **marketing** significance of the findings. Now that you have the information, so what? What do you do with it, and how do you use it to make decisions?

As we've said, by statistical significance, we mean the statement of how much of a difference you must see in two specific numbers—say 45% versus 51%—to say the two numbers are really different in the real world (or at least 95 times out of 100). But what is **more important** is what is the marketing relevance of the difference. It may well be true that an average rating of 6.1 on a ten-point scale is statistically different from an average rating of 6.5. But what are we going to do with that information? How are we going to make a different conclusion from one average rating over the other?

Many years ago there was a company, which came up with the idea of selling advertising space on park benches and went around the country trying to convince advertising agencies to put their client's ads on their park benches. Of course, the first question an advertising agency is likely to ask is "how do you know that advertising on park benches makes any difference?"

To a researcher, this is an obvious cry for a controlled experiment, or what is known as a Pre and Post test. You do a survey to measure the recall of a particular brand name, then you put the name on the benches, and do another survey a short time later. If you get 10% of the people naming the brand—or recalling a specific message only on the benches—in the Pre Wave prior to the park bench advertising, and you get 40% after the ads have been on the benches for a few weeks, then you can probably conclude that the park benches caused the increase in the awareness level of the brand.

So, the park bench company did the usual survey. One of the brands had a 0% awareness level in the Pre wave (so far so good), and in the Post wave it had 2%. Now, anyone, even non-statisticians, should be able to see that if the Post recall is only 2%, that does not say much for the impact of the park bench advertising. The presenter of this study must have heard such a comment before, because he was prepared with an argument: "our statisticians tell us that a two percentage point increase is a significant increase."

Ok, so it is. So what? Would you invest in a park bench ad campaign if only 2% remembered it? This is a perfect example of how statistical significance does not translate into marketing significance. And this does not even get to the second observation from this Pre and Post research in that even if brand name awareness did increase, does that increase in awareness translate into anything else such as a more favorable attitude towards the brand or an increased likelihood to purchase it. All of us have seen many advertising campaigns that increased awareness but had no impact on anything else.

On the other hand, sometimes you can translate a statistically significant finding into marketing significance. Many people may remember the "Pepsi challenge" a few years ago when people were served a unlabeled sample of Pepsi Cola and an unlabeled sample of Coca-Cola, with the heavily reported findings that "people prefer Pepsi." (If you lived in Atlanta, you probably never heard this advertising, because Pepsi did not originally run it in Atlanta, the home of Coca Cola, figuring that the longer Coke management was not daily exposed to it, the longer they could run it without incurring their wrath.)

What the Pepsi challenge ads did not say, or if they said so it was in such small print that it was hardly noticeable, was that the actual preference was something like 51% prefer Pepsi to 49% who preferred Coke under these conditions: (1) if the product was served at a certain temperature, and (2) if the taster only had a sip or two of the products for comparison. (Because in such a "sip test," where only a sip or two of a beverage is consumed, the sweeter drink will often win. This does not mean that if you drank an entire bottle of a sweet beverage, that you would prefer it, but you well might like it best if you only had a sip or two.)

If both of these conditions were not met, then the reported preferences for Pepsi did not hold. And that doesn't even take into account the brand name of Pepsi versus Coca Cola, in that if people know the brand of product they are tasting, their knowledge of that brand name can affect preferences.

Another point to keep in mind is that if the sample size is large enough, almost any difference will be statistically significant.

In the soft drink example, a sample of 3000 was necessary to show a 51/49% preference, which was statistically significant, but for all practical purposes, it's really pretty much the same as 50/50.

If we do an employee survey, and there are 43,000 employees who respond, then even a one percentage point difference will be a statistically significant difference, but that does not mean such a difference has any real meaning in decision making.

16.

What you don't know can hurt you.

What you don't know can hurt you in a lot of ways. If you don't know the right technique to use for a research project, the wrong technique can cause you to draw the wrong conclusions. If you do not know how to use a technique, the same thing can happen. If you don't know how to analyze the findings, ditto.

Often no one ever knows that the wrong questions were asked, because there is no one to speak out. The client has hired the research firm to ask the questions, so the client often does not know. And if the researcher knows, he is not telling.

In one particular instance, an in-home use test of a seasoning product, Butter Buds, appeared to show that while initial usage of the product was low, if the product stayed in the home for a longer period of time, usage increased. So the agency concluded that the product should be introduced and then extensive advertising should be run to increase usage once it was in the home.

And what was the conclusion that led to this fallacy? Simply this. When callback interviews were conducted after two weeks of test usage, the product was used an average of 3.1 times a week. In this test, consumers were offered the chance to keep the product another week after which time another callback interview was conducted. After this second two-week usage test, usage increased to 4.3 times a week. Obviously, the product grew on people as they continued to use it. Wrong!!!

Here's what happened. In the first test of 300 people who used it 3.1 times a week, some 30% used it only once. So when the first callback interview was conducted and everyone was asked if they wanted it for another two weeks, only 220 people continued in the test. The second callback was made to these 220 people. Thus, the second callback was made only among people who liked the product, and those who, if their answers had been separated from the non-users after week one, would have shown an average usage of 4.9 times a week. In reality, even those on the second callback were using it less than they had been using it after the first week. The researcher's report drew exactly the opposite conclusion. It was only when a new researcher joined the agency that this error was discovered.

Or suppose you fail to ask the right question, and as a result you draw the wrong conclusion. This is not as hard to do as it might seem, and it can have serious consequences.

Here's a classic case. Say you have a new formula for a well-known brand and conduct a taste test comparing the new formula to the current formula. In the test, 62% of the 1000 tasters like the product with the new formula, and 38% prefer the product with the current formula. Consequently, you replace the old product with the new one and run right into a sales disaster requiring the old product to be brought back.

This is the result of not asking the right question in the research. What's the missing question? Simply this: you failed to ask the 38% of the people who liked the current product if they would continue to buy the new product, or if instead, they might switch to a competitive brand. Again, statistical significance is not marketing significance.

What you don't know about the interviewing and data processing process can also hurt you.

If you don't know that a voting intention question was preceded by a question rating the candidate, you don't know that the voting intentions were biased by that question.

If you don't know that voting intentions vary based on the interaction of the race of the interviewer and the race of the respondent, you don't know how to determine the true voting intentions if there is a black candidate in the race. (White respondents overstate their intentions to vote for an African-American when talking to black interviewers so as to not appear prejudiced.)

If you don't know that data entry operators average a 2% error rate in keystrokes, then when you are entering data from paper questionnaires, you might be tempted to use a firm which charges less for data entry but does not do 100% validation of keystrokes.

17.

The best marketing research reports don't look like marketing research reports.

I t's no wonder why management consulting is a $200+ billion dollar industry, while marketing research is less than $10 billion. And it's not because management consultants are necessarily smarter (although they may be since their revenues are so much higher), but rather because management consultants know how to talk to the CEO, the CFO, and other top management. Management consultants talk dollars, while marketing researchers talk percentages, mean ratings, and statistical significance. And it's dollars on which a company's top management is evaluated. Who ever got fired because of a mean rating?

Unless specifically blocked by the client, all research reports should contain a summary of the findings, the conclusions drawn from that summary, and recommendations. If anyone wants to wade through the pages and pages of computer prints, they should be available. But don't include them unless the client asks for them. It's easier for them to call you and ask you to look into it. And it will probably take less time than explaining what all the computer printout columns are and what they mean.

Write short reports and put the conclusions up front. Even print them on a different color paper if you need to, so they can be easily found.

Don't write an 859 page report, including a 59 page summary, and expect anyone to read it and come away with any real findings. (I am not making this up.)

Write short reports with less data but more information. Or as the newspaper editor said to the new copy boy: "Cut this story in half but don't leave out a word."

18.

Don't think you can find out why somebody does something just by asking them why they do it.

Another way to state this is, "don't let questions do all the work." It is essential, of course, to ask questions in marketing research. But good research is more than asking questions. You have to ask the right questions, in the right way.

It's quite common in a survey to ask someone why they do something, or why they do not do something. Now, these may be good questions to get at the basic dimensions driving attitudes and decisions, especially in a focus group, but asking such questions assumes (1) people know why they do things and (2) they will tell you. Either one or both of these assumptions can easily be dangerous.

It's particularly instructive to compare what people **say** is important in a category purchase decision to what is **really** important. For instance, when asking about restaurants, people will say that cleanliness is important. For airlines, they will agree that safety is important, and for a bank, financial stability is always stated to be important. Yet this does not mean that if a restaurant advertises cleanliness, an airline advertises safety, or a bank advertises financial stability, it will gain business, because while important in a *category*, they may not drive *brand* decisions. Perhaps all restaurants are seen as clean, all airlines safe, and all banks sound. The category attribute is not a differentiating measure for a brand.

We define "what people say" as Stated Importance: we asked the question, and they told us (stated) their answer. But what people say may not give much insight, because in such a situation, answers tend to be what makes the respondent sound like an intelligent con-sumer ("I recycle all my grocery shopping bags," "I look for healthy foods when shopping," "I want to find the safest car I can buy.")

A better way to examine what is really important is to see what really drives where someone shops, or Derived Importance, meaning how specific attributes (such as convenience or low prices) correlate with an overall brand rating. For example, if someone rates an electronics store high on "low prices" and that is where they shop, this says that the "low prices" attribute is strongly suggestive of why someone shops there. If that same store is rated low on "free stereo hookups," this says that attribute is not important in where they shop. In other words, we derive the importance not by asking but by discovering how it relates to the overall brand rating or where they shop.

Comparisons of what people say (Stated Importance) compared to how they actually behave (Derived Importance) is often very instructive. There are four combinations of stated and derived importance, often shown in a map with the following four quadrants (plot the derived importance vertically and the stated importance horizontally):

* **Key Drivers** are those attributes that are high in Stated Importance as well as Derived Importance. Outstanding performance in both areas will produce strong sales. An example for a retail store might be "value for the money," "knowledgeable sales people," and "high quality products." People say these are important, and they do help determine where someone shops.

* **Price of Entry** are attributes high in Stated Importance but low in Derived Importance. They are the crucial but not sufficient characteristics in that they must be present to ensure consumer choice or satisfaction, but do not differentiate among competitors. In the retail store example, these might be attributes such as "low prices" and "good selection of brands." Every big box electronics retailer says they have low prices and a wide selection because

people say it is important, but just saying that won't help much. It's the price of entry into the category.

* **Latent Motivators** are those characteristics people may not admit are important (such as "sales people who make you feel comfortable") but in reality have a high correlation to where one shops.

* **Low Priority** items are those attributes low in Stated and Derived Importance, and thus not necessary to emphasize. An example might be "free hookup of stereo equipment," an attribute which people say is not important and in reality may not make any difference in a store where one shops (i.e., low correlation with the overall rating of the store).

Now that we know Derived Importance, we can compare that to how the brand actually performs; that is Importance versus Performance. Often times a brand will perform well on attributes that are not very important and perform poorly on attributes that really drive sales and share.

We once did such a study for Kingsberry Homes, a
modular home manufacturer, whose market was inde-
pendent homebuilders. Of all the 20 or 30 attributes on
which Kingsberry Homes was rated, including quality of
materials, on-time delivery, prompt response when you
have a problem, etc., do you know what was their highest rated attribute?

The building supplier's printed t-shirts they gave
out to the builders! The copy on the t-shirts read,
"With Kingsberry Homes, you get it up quickly."
Another version read, "It takes a stud to build a
Kingsberry home."

Another reason a survey participant may not be
able to answer the question of why they have **not** done
something is that they really don't have a reason, or
they have never thought about it enough to have a reason.

That is the kind of response you get when you ask
someone why he or she has not been to particular

restaurant, bought a particular brand of milk, or not bought a certain automobile make. The most common answer is usually:

"I just haven't."

"I never thought about it."

"No particular reason."

"It's not convenient."

Not very helpful answers are they? And even the last answer of "it's not convenient," doesn't necessarily mean the restaurant is not convenient. What the answer could really mean might be something like, "It is not enough of a good product to drive out of my way for," or, "I don't know enough about it to make a special trip." In other words, an answer of not convenient (as well as other responses of this type) has nothing to do with convenience at all. It is an easy answer to give and a harder one to interpret.

In a focus group for a particular fast food restaurant chain, the client had given specific instructions that all

people recruited for the groups must work or live within three miles of one of their restaurants. This was a valid
request, because if the restaurant in question really was
inconveniently located, opinions from those participants
would not be as useful as are opinions from those who
pass by the restaurant every day and have the opportunity for trial and repeat business.

As the discussion from the first group progressed,
the client sitting behind the mirror began to get con-
cerned, and even questioned the recruiting for the
group, because at least half the participants were saying
that this restaurant was not located anywhere around
where they lived or worked. The research firm immediately began checking the home and work addresses of
participants against a list of the client's restaurants and
found that at least one restaurant was convenient to
every respondent. What was happening was that the
restaurants were constructed so that they actually
"blended in" along the highway, and many people just
did not know they were there. Or they had such low
visibility or low importance to the group participant that

the store never entered their mind. "Oh, yes, there is one right where I live. I go by it every day. I just did not think of it when we were talking about fast food restaurants because I had a bad experience there one time and would not go back."

One of the most common questions that people are often tempted to ask are questions about liking or disliking the advertising. It is rare that a researcher should ask about, or should care about, whether or not the consumer likes or dislikes the advertising. Whether or not someone likes or dislikes the advertising is rarely important in determining if they will buy the product. Of course, there may be some ads that are so nauseating that the viewer is tempted to say that they would never buy the product due to the terrible advertising, but this is rare. Most often, if the consumer does not like the ads, that person is not in the target audience for the ads in the first place.

The same goes for packaging. It is virtually useless to ask if someone likes the package, at least from an aesthetic standpoint. (Functionality is another matter.) Rather, a good package does two things:

a) It stands out on the shelf or in the display.

b) It communicates the relevant points about the product from the package.

Naming research is another activity where the right questions should be asked. Liking or disliking a name is rarely relevant. Rather, a good name for a product has a number of characteristics, such as being easy to pronounce and memorable. A good name does not necessarily have to relate to the product, although in a test of a new name, those which relate better will score better. If there had been a test of the names Burger King and McDonald's years before either chain began, most name tests would have said that Burger King is a better name because it more easily tells what the product category is. After all, what does McDonald's mean for a hamburger restaurant. A name is what you make it. Therefore, McDonald's is certainly at least as good a name as Burger King.

Be careful with advertising, name, and package testing. Consumers will typically act logically in answering your questions, yet advertising, name, and packaging raise emotional as well as logical issues.

19.

People lie when talking to researchers.

Most of the time they do not consciously lie. But often, since they don't know the answer, they will just give you one, and that may or may not be the real answer, just like teenagers (and others) in a mall survey will make up phone numbers if asked to provide one. (We wouldn't do that ourselves would we, when the cashier asks for our phone number, because we know that might put us on a mailing list? Of course not!)

Most major purchase or behavioral decisions involve some degree of thought. However, the responses to most surveys—or especially telephone or mall interceptions—come out of the blue. You are walking through the mall and are stopped to answer a few questions. Or, you are just sitting down at home to watch a TV program, and someone calls you on the phone to find out how you decide what brand of tires to buy, or at what store you would buy a washing machine, or the next time you go out to eat where will you go. And while these top of mind answers are important, they may not be in depth enough to provide meaningful information.

People also overestimate what they will do, especially when it comes to purchase intentions. Just because 30% of the sample says they will "definitely" buy the product, does not mean that 30% will actually buy it. Buying intentions are one the most common answers subject to overstatement. Not only are buying intentions overstated, in a concept test where buying intentions are asked, the researcher has generated 100% awareness of the new product because every respondent has been shown the concept. In the real world, the advertising would only generate so much awareness, and an adjustment must be made for that. Further, a product will not get into distribution where 100% of the target audience can purchase it, so an adjustment must also be made for estimated distribution levels. And since some advertising may be more powerful than other creative approaches, there must be some adjustment for "average" versus "superb" creative. One research firm, which predicts the ultimate sales success of a new product, simply adds 20% to their estimated revenue if the advertising agency can provide "superb" creative.

Some people lie on purpose because not to do so would reflect badly on them. Who wants to tell a stranger that he does not regularly use mouthwash, or that she only brushes her teeth once a day, or that she does not read ingredient labels? And certainly many more people than actually clip coupons say they do, because how foolish would you look if you don't pay attention to good values?

With a little background, you can do a simple experiment. From easily available reference resources based on surveys, look up the proportion of adults who say they use a mouthwash every day and multiply an average amount per usage times the number of adults in the country, times 365 days. Then compare the actual amount of mouthwash sold in this country. Who would like to bet that the projection of how much people say they use is a multiple of the actual amount sold?

The trick is finding out when they are lying and when they are telling the truth. That's the challenge of a good marketing researcher.

Sometimes people lie and don't realize it. They talk in a focus group about how much they are cutting down on junk food while reaching for the potato chips and soft drinks on the table. They say they are not influenced by advertising, but they are. After all, advertising works, or no one would do it.

A shopper may say a supermarket is not conveniently located, but she may really mean it doesn't provide enough benefits for her to make a left turn at the traffic light. Convenience is relative. You might find it convenient to drive ten miles out of your way if only one store had the special item you wanted.

20.

There is no particular course of study needed to become a good marketing researcher.

Want to be an engineer, get an engineering degree. To become a teacher, get a degree in teaching. Want to be a lawyer, go to law school.

Want to be a marketing researcher? Study just about anything, or just start as an interviewer working in a data collection facility, and work your way up.

Now, as a famous TV personality might say, "Not that there is anything wrong with that." And I happen to agree completely. Certainly, there are incompetent engineers who have an engineering degree, bad teachers who have a teaching certificate, and bad architects with architectural degrees who don't know how to put up exit signs in parking decks.

Looking to hire a good marketing researcher? What kind of a person do you look for? Until a few years ago, there was not even any recognized course of study to become a market researcher. True, you could take one or two courses in marketing research, all taught from an academic standpoint, but no one really learned about marketing research in college. Rather, it was not until you got out into the real world that you really got educated in marketing research.

Even today, there are only four graduate schools where you can get an advanced degree in marketing research, called an MMR. (Master of Marketing Research.) These four schools are the University of Georgia (which started the first school), the University of Wisconsin, the University of Texas/ Arlington, and Southern Illinois. However, with programs graduating less than 30 students per school per year, it means that most researchers come from other disciplines.

The good news, and I mean this sincerely, is that it really doesn't matter the school you went to, your background, or your course of study, **as long as** (and this "as long as" is crucial) you have the traits that a good market researcher has. And since these traits cut across all disciplines, if you have these traits, you can have a degree—or not even have a degree—and be a good market researcher.

Simply stated, these traits include (indeed, a good market researcher **must** have): common sense, a strong sense of reasoning, creative thinking, and excellent written and verbal communication skills. The mind of Leonardo da Vinci, we call it. If you can think like da Vinci, you will in most cases be an excellent market researcher. Such thinking was excellently summarized in a book by Thomas Gelb, "How to Think Like Leonardo da Vinci" as follows:

1. *Curiosita* — a curious approach to life
   and quest for continuous learning.

2. *Dimostrazione* — a commitment to test
   knowledge through experience.

3. *Sensazione* — the continual refinement
   of the senses.

4. *Sfumato* — a willingness to embrace
   ambiguity, paradox, and uncertainty.

5. *Arte/Scienza* — the blending of art and
   science, logic and imagination, whole brain
   thinking.

6. *Corporalita* — the cultivation of grace,
   ambidexterity, fitness, and poise.

7. *Connessione* — recognition of how everything
   is connected. (As Edmund Wilson, the noted
   biologist, would say, consilience.)

The student who scores a perfect 800 or 1600 on his or her SAT score might want to re-think a career as a marketing researcher. The University of Georgia MMR school has found, in fact, that if you are "too smart" with numbers and statistics and in math, you can actually hurt your chances of becoming a good market research manager. A good researcher must be able to think and communicate, not just know how to manipulate the numbers.

21.

Beware of any research if the findings can be reported by just one number.

We call this the fallacy of single number research. One characteristic which marketing research has, perhaps unique relative to other parts of the advertising process, is the capacity to be both overly complex and overly simplistic at the same time. We have all had experience with the overly complex research project: the hundreds of pages of computer printouts, scores of tabular data, and a summary so long that sometimes a summary of the summary must be written. Like many a marketing plan, the value of the research often seems to be in how heavy a document can be produced, rather than in answering the key question of what the numbers mean.

Often it seems that the longer a report is, the more confusing it is, and the harder it is to answer the question for which it was conducted in the first place. Yet, that is generally all that top management is interested in. We are not going to comment further about this kind of research except to have sympathy for the marketing manager and advertising agency who must decipher what it means. Rather, we would like to comment on the opposite kind of report, one that many people think is easy to understand, but often isn't. We call this single number research.

By single number research we mean any research that produces a single number, which purports to summarize the findings and make it easy to make a decision. Here are some examples:

A day-after-recall (DAR) test. "Our commercial got a 30 and the average for the category is only 21."

A product test. "We are preferred 2 to 1 over the competition."

A concept test. "This one is a real winner. 85% say they will buy the product."

An ad recall study. "Our ads are recalled by 55% of cat owners."

Reduced to statements like this, management decisions are easy. Use the commercial that scored twice the norm. Change to the new formula preferred by 65%. Introduce the new product that most people say they are going to buy. And continue to run the advertising because most people say they remember it.

We reject this kind of simplistic reasoning. Sure it makes the decision easy. And that's one reason it is easy to sell. Top management does not have to understand how the technique works, just that they got a good number. Yet is it that simple? We think not. There is no single number by which a commercial can be adequately (or magically) evaluated. Of course, certain elements can be tested, and we can see if a particular message is communicated, if it was remembered, and if it was relevant to the buying decision. A commercial might have a high day-after-recall (DAR) score. But what is the DAR among the target audience? (Most standardized commercial testing services test among the general adult population, one reason being that they do multiple tests at a time, and it's too difficult (i.e., too expensive) to do a single test among households who (a) buy potato chips (b) own a dog and (c) are prospects for life insurance. So commercials for all three brands are tested among women 21-65, for example, with no category usage qualifications at all.

Another mis-use of single numbers is in ad recall. We need to know more, for example, than the observation that 65% say they recall advertising for the brand. What do they recall? How much of the recall is the related message, or copy points, rather than execution? Is it remembered by the right people?

Recently, we tested a commercial with strong recall; however, 85% of those who remembered the commercial recalled an element of the commercial's execution (what was said in the commercial) rather than the message the commercial was trying to impart. Now, some people would be happy with any commercial with a high recall, but with some exceptions, commercials which do a good job in selling the product focus more on the selling points, or reason to purchase, than focus on the execution. The advertising graveyard is littered with expensive, fancy commercials that focus attention on the commercial rather than the message.

An automobile commercial several years ago featured dolls driving a toy car. It had great recall of the commercial (the single number fallacy again) and great word of mouth, because everyone was talking about the commercial with the toy car, but few remembered the brand of car being advertised; in fact, the particular model of that car was not even on the market when the commercial was run. So in spite of the commercial being written up in the press, and Time magazine saying it was the best commercial of the year, the commercial was ultimately withdrawn when their dealers started complaining of lower sales of their brand. But it got a good test score!

An advertiser may like the fact that people remember the commercial, but the purpose of advertising is not to generate commercial recall. The purpose of advertising is to communicate a relevant, important message to the target audience. If it does this, the commercial is a success. Whether or not people say they remember the commercial responsible for this is irrelevant.

In a product test the researchers reported a 50/50 preference for the new formula of cleaning product, and one might conclude that either formula could be used since as many people preferred the old as the new formula. A closer examination, however, showed that 80% of current users preferred the current product, and an equally strong 80% of competitive brand users preferred the new formula. What to do depends upon the marketing objectives: is it more important to keep current users, or gain new ones?

The net of all this is to be careful with single number research. It may hide more than it shows. And the simple conclusion may not be all that simple.

22.

Focusing on just part of a study can lead you to the wrong conclusions.

ecause so many questions in a survey are asked among segments of the sample who respond in certain ways to previous questions, it is common to show answers as a percentage of those asked the question. Sounds logical, doesn't it? If you ask which of two products are preferred and the reason for the preference, would you not show the reasons for preference among those having that preference?

Well, no, you wouldn't. Or at least you shouldn't, because it will be misinterpreted.

Let's say you have two brands for soft drinks, A and B. You correctly blind taste test the two products.

(Skipping for now if you should do it in a mall where each person takes a sip or two of each, or give each a bottle to drink at home, because which technique you use can affect the results!)

And the preference out of 300 people comes out 65% prefer A, and 35% prefer B. OK so far. But now you ask why those who prefer A do prefer A, and why those who prefer B prefer B. A perfectly normal (and wrong) way would be to show the reasons for preference like this:

	Why Prefer A	**Why Prefer B**
(number who prefer)	(195)	(105)
Reasons:		
Tastes better	50%	70%
More fizz	40	35
Prettier color	60	30

You show this to the brand manager, and he says: "You are telling me that more people prefer B for taste than A? B is a terrible product, and in fact two out of three prefer A. How can that be? How can 70% of B people prefer it for taste when only 50% prefer A for taste?"

The answer, of course, is that there are twice as many people who prefer A for taste than B. But you percentaged the answers **to those who preferred B.** And while it is true that B preferrers are more likely to prefer B for taste, there are not as many of them.

Here's how the table should be presented. It's how all reasons for preference answers should be presented.

Reasons for Preference
(300 respondents)

	Prefer A	Prefer B
Overall preference	65%	35%
Taste	33	24
Fizz	26	12
Color	20	21

Now the data are easy to read and interpret, and you don't have to explain a percentage of a percentage. Brand A is the preferred product because more people like the taste and fizz of A than like the taste and fizz of B.

Far too often, percents are shown as percents of percents. In addition to showing percents of the total, we need to be more cognizant of the totals in most questions. For example, the level of ad recall should be based on the total sample, not those aware of the brand.

Copy point recall, if it is presented as a percentage of those who recall the ads, should also be presented as a percentage of the total sample.

Trial of a brand should be percentaged to the total sample; if it's percentaged as a proportion of those aware, then that statistic should be called **conversion** of awareness to trial, not **trial.**

23.

Don't judge a research report by how long or thick or heavy it is, or by how many people were interviewed, or by how many fancy statistical techniques were used.

Over the years, vast improvements have been made in research techniques and design, in sampling, in statistical analysis of data, and in numerous quality controls that affect the validity and projectability of marketing research. Some of this gets into reports and makes them longer. But longer reports are not necessarily any better.

Research is not (or should not be) bought by the pound. Any research report, regardless of the number of people interviewed, the number of techniques, or the number of questions asked, should be reducible to a one or two page summary executive overview. The report itself should be clearly written and easy to read, including conclusions and implications. It is this type of report that management has both the time and desire to read and the confidence to accept. Anything short of that is a waste of research time and money, regardless of how heavy the report is.

Several factors help make reports longer than they should be.

*Indiscriminate use of fancy tools, particularly the multivariate ones, may confuse rather than enlighten.

*Letting questions do all the work. Research is more than asking questions. How simple is it to ask someone in a package test if she likes the package? Or if a consumer does not use a product, ask him why not. Even those are the wrong questions. Yet, they are often asked, and their answers are reported. But just because you get answers does not mean they are valid answers. Answers to wrong questions hardly constitute analysis.

*Reporting what happened rather than what it means. Too much research text simply repeats numbers in an accompanying table. Yet, we assume that our readers can read too. It is more important to comment on the marketing significance of the numbers. How are we better off by knowing the answers?

There are no "jumbo sizes" or "super sizes" in marketing research. You should interview only the number of people necessary to make the right decision. You should only ask the questions to which you need to know the answers. You want a report only long enough to learn what to do as a result of the research.

Don't be impressed by the length of the report, or how many banners of computer printouts it has. Unless your job is checking the tables to be sure they are correct, or if you only purchased data tables and not analysis, you should not even bother with cross-tabs. That's what you should pay a research firm to do.

Nor does the size of the research firm matter, as long as it can deliver what is promised. Some large research firms provide excellent products and services. Some small firms do the same thing. Don't be impressed by how many employees the firm has, or how many reports it has written, or how many clients it has, or who their clients are. Sometimes there is an inverse relationship between quality and service and size of company.

24.

Your research will be better accepted if it agrees with the opinions of whoever is paying for the research.

I f you have this kind of client, you need a new client. However, it is often true that the acceptance as to the validity of a piece of marketing research can well depend on whether or not the person paying for the research accepts and believes what you have to say.

As much as anyone else, marketing and brand managers and company presidents like research to validate their own feelings and beliefs. That's why a focus group can be judged good or bad depending upon how well the group likes the product manager's new product, regardless of whether or not the group was properly recruited and the moderator did a good job.

If the research leads to one conclusion regarding a new product idea, and if the champion of that product agrees with the research, then there is no stopping the new product, even if the conclusions drawn from the research are wrong. We have seen this happen time and again with disastrous results.

We have seen:

— A brand manager who did not understand why consumers did not buy more of his cleaning product because this brand manager used a can a week. ("But Steve, you get it free!")
— A new formula introduced to replace a strong selling product because key executives in the company grew up in a country where this type of product was preferred.

— A food product representing only 10% of a
company's sales, but the President liked the
product and refused to believe research
showing consumers would just as soon buy
the cheaper product. (That's what the 10% of
sales statistic was trying to say.)

— A new service concept introduced when the
concept had a 0% Top Box "definitely buy"
score (our norm is 30% for successful
products) because not to introduce the
product would cause the agency to lose an
account scheduled to spend over a million
dollars in advertising. ("The research shows
that most people are not negative, and after
all, it has been successful in Canada.")
Footnote: they introduced the product
anyway, and lost over a million dollars doing
so before pulling the product off the market.

— A food products company whose R&D
director refused to believe that consumers did
not like her company's product. ("We drink it
all the time in the plant; how can you say

consumers don't like the product?") This
R&D director was so adamant about not
believing the research that she hired another
research firm to repeat the test and told
neither firm about the other test. This second
firm, of course, drew the same conclusion,
and eventually the formula was changed.

— An advertising agency that did not like the
researcher's report saying their new
commercial was ineffective, so they did not
use that research firm again for six years.

— A dairy products company who used to do
taste testing using their advertising agency's
employees. When, time after time, the client's
products lost to competition, the client simply
stopped asking the agency to do the taste
testing.

25.

The more you know about marketing research, the more you need to know about marketing research.

At least in the area of most sciences, the more you study, learn, and experience, the more you will know about your topic of interest, your life's work. You don't know less about engineering after you've been in it for 20 years. You don't know less about nuclear energy the longer you work in it.

Marketing research does not fit this pattern. The longer you are in marketing research, the more complex it becomes. The more you do, the more you learn when to break the rules, when to draw conclusions opposite from what the data appear to say, and the less sure you are of what the data mean.

And the more you know about marketing research, the more you learn that a lot of other people don't know much about marketing research either. From the new hire at The Pillsbury Company who once suggested that the company's cherry frozen turnover be withdrawn from the market because it only got a 7.2 on a 9 point scale, whereas apple got an 8.2 and blueberry a 7.9, to the belief that you can test advertising in focus groups, there's enough lack of information to go around for everybody.

The more marketing research you do, the more you begin to draw on your own experience about what the data mean. "Yes, it's right in the table, but it's not right." "I know people said that, but...." "This concept came out on the bottom, but it's actually the best one." "Even though 62% of the sample preferred this new formula, we should not introduce it." And on and on and on.

But that's good. It's good because we are not slaves to numbers. Because we can put art and science, left brain and right brain, together. Because we learn over the years what works and what does not work. Because we can take all we know and help our clients build better, more profitable brands that make a difference in peoples' lives.

That's what makes marketing research so much fun.

The Future of Marketing Research

L ike all industries, marketing research has and needs to change with the times. Over the last seventy years or so, marketing research has gone through several phases:

A. The 1930-60's.

This was the golden age of development of marketing research, where once well-known researchers made their mark, and whose companies enabled marketing research to become more widely used: first by advertising agencies and consumer packaged goods, then by extensions into other products and services, such as health care, financial services, and other institutions.

B. The 1960-90's.

During this time frame, marketing research continued to expand, with the availability of sophisticated analytical tools such as factor analysis, segmentation, perceptual mapping, conjoint, and other mathematical models.

C. The 1990's to the present.

Research is experiencing two parallel developments at the current time. First is the desire to have everything faster. Fax machines, voice mail, the PC, and the Internet, in conjunction with today's fast paced environment, means there is less time than ever to conduct and report good research. We see no reason that this time pressure will not continue.

The other development, the most important one for clients and researchers, is the increased focus on marketing *intelligence* as opposed to marketing *research*. Sure, the research steps are still here. But, relatively few, if any, new techniques have been developed. Rather, it is becoming increasingly more important for researchers to be able to communicate not what the data *say*, but what the data *mean*. Sophisticated research techniques are great if they help explain what is happening. But they should not be done for show, rather for analytical insight.

Research has to be more than "interesting." It must be actionable. It must be conducted among the proper target audience, with the right questions asked the right way, and properly analyzed and reported.

If one takes the sum of numbers in a typical research project, such as the computer tabulations cross-tabulated in multiples of nineteen different ways (a typical computer printout has 19 columns of data), it is obvious that far less than 5% of the data from a typical study is ever used.

Why do we ask the other 95%? Part of the answer is that we don't know in advance which 5% will be useful. But another part of the answer is that researchers often get in the habit of asking too many questions because that's what they are accustomed to do. How many times are certain demographics asked, and nothing is done with them? How many times are the same questions asked over and over.

Research reports suffer from, on the one hand, being under analyzed. On the other hand, many are overanalyzed because too many improper conclusions are drawn from the data.

Current Issues in Marketing Research

As marketing research grows and as more and more people enter the field, the body of knowledge expands, as do the problems and opportunities. Here are some of the critical issues facing the industry over the years ahead:

Do we know what we're doing?

Many contributed to marketing research from its late-1800s beginnings to its early—to mid-1900s development. Yet, researchers still have much to learn. Many of the things pioneer Alfred Politz said over 50 years ago are ignored today. Take this statement from a 1955 interview:

> "Subjective importance of your claim is most important. Then your claim must be believable and unique."

But we often read today that: "People like the ads." Politz said that it was a myth in marketing research "that advertising research should be directed to determine which ads are liked. ...The most effective advertising makes consumers like the product, think of the product more favorably without the advertising."

So, one of the critical issues in marketing research is that many people still do not know how to measure the effectiveness of advertising. Many don't know what good advertising is, what marketing research can and cannot do, or when to do or not do it.

The growing concern about privacy and legal issues

The nation has a growing concern over privacy. Ann Landers, for example, has told her readers not to answer surveys over the phone.

Caller ID is an outgrowth of this. The growing concern over privacy has spawned many new laws, but fortunately for the research industry, no significant state or federal laws have been passed in the last five years that have had a negative effect on marketing research.

The growth of telemarketing

There are over 500 million telemarketing calls made each week. Coupled with the growing concern over privacy, the refusal rate on telephone surveys has increased and often is greater than 50%.

The good news is that there is no key group of people who consistently refuse to answer. Some people refuse because a particular survey is inconvenient at the time but answer other times.

The increased use of marketing research for entertainment for its own sake

It is not necessary, or wise, to research everything. How many times have you seen a survey result in the paper and asked yourself, "Who cares?"

The misuse of marketing research.

"Sugging," or selling under the guise of marketing research, and "frugging," or fund raising under the guise of marketing research, are examples of major misuse.

Sugging is now illegal due to the Telemarketing Fraud Act of 1996, but, of course, this does not mean it has been stopped.

The overuse of focus groups is one other misuse of marketing research, and call-in polls are another.

The advancement of science more than art

Marketing research is both art and science. There is an art in knowing how to ask questions and whom to ask, as well as to knowing how to interpret the answers. This art has not improved over the years and may have actually gotten worse.

However, the science of marketing research has improved. Technology has improved techniques, primarily to get information faster. Examples include the CATI system, and the ability of computers to produce crosstabs, multivariates and modeling.

But where in all of this is better data on which to make better decisions? What major new techniques have been used, much less developed, during the last 20 years or so?

The lack of training for new researchers and the shortage of good researchers

There are fewer and fewer training programs in marketing research. In addition, companies have downsized, and training programs by advertisers and ad agencies have suffered cutbacks.

Many of the major consumer packaged goods companies used to start newly hired researchers (even with a Masters Degree) by writing questionnaires and then going out to a neighborhood to knock on doors and ask the questions. They would then tabulate the responses to their surveys and write a report. Trainees hated this work, but it made them all better researchers.

This also relates to the next critical issue:

The continuing gap between academics and business

There are only four universities that offer a graduate program in marketing research. Historically, these programs are primarily focused on training people to be consumer packaged goods researchers in large multinational companies. However, this is changing so that now researchers are trained in business-to-business as well as consumer services research.

There are basic topics schools need to teach, such as common sense, thinking and ethics. Those techniques can be learned. But where is the emphasis on critical thinking and report writing skills?

The emphasis on speed over everything else

Everyone wants things faster and cheaper. If a researcher could have one more day on a project, even if the project lasted six weeks, that one more day could add 20% or more in value to the study. Yet it always seems we never have that extra day.

At least a few years ago, we could say, "It's in the mail," and have a day longer to work on it.

The value of marketing research as investment

These are increasing developments in determining the return on investments (ROI) in marketing research. In other words, if we do this research, how much return on the research dollars will we receive? More work should be done in this area.

The need to educate buyers on how to buy marketing research

Often, buying marketing research—that is, deciding what provider to use—is delegated down to those who lack the knowledge or ability to make the right decision. Too many think all research providers are the same, don't know how to evaluate price and quality and always take the lowest bid.

Good marketing research may or may not be expensive. But good marketing research is always a good investment and a good value.

Marketing Research in the Future

Marketing research is a multibillion industry, practiced by more than 7,500 marketing research firms as well as thousands of adverting agencies and users of marketing research. So one might think that now everyone has it right—that there are sound scientific principles of how, when and where to do marketing research and what it all means.

In scientific fields, basic advancements in knowledge gradually change what we know about our world. In marketing research, it is the individual's advancement that contributes to the understanding of why people behave as they do and how they form attitudes about products and services.

I would argue that there are more advancements in marketing research knowledge of the individual marketing researcher throughout his or her career than in the field as a whole for any time period. Yet for the most part, this knowledge remains with the individual; there is no network or clearinghouse for information.

Marketing research is very much like advertising, and to quote an old saying, "Half my advertising is wasted, but I don't know which half." In physics, numbers mean what they mean. The marketing research numbers can mean what the market researcher wants them to mean.

Sometimes, marketing research should be done, but isn't. Other times it should not be done, but is. And perhaps more often, the wrong kind of research is done for the wrong reasons and the wrong conclusions are drawn. We see this in the lack of success of hundreds of products, most of which, at least if they are from major advertisers, ultimately fail to achieve expected levels of success.

In reviewing marketing research over the last 25 years, we are struck by the observation that most changes have been in speed, not techniques. Twenty-five years ago, overnight delivery did not exist. Nor did fax machines or personal computers. Nor e-mail or the World Wide Web. Virtually all advances in marketing research have been to get information faster and, at the same time, wanting it cheaper.

Perhaps we shouldn't expect techniques to change. After all, has human behavior changed in the last few thousand years? We should expect, however, a better understanding of behavior. More than 25 years ago, Alfred Politz, one of the great researchers of all time, talked about how advertising should be measured based on the importance, uniqueness and believability of the message.

Yet today, we still have advertising evaluated on how much one "likes" the advertising. Much of the information we should know has already been discovered but not communicated.

It's certainly true that marketing research is generally accepted as a worthwhile business effort. The challenge comes in applying it at a local or company level, because, for the most part, "hard" dollars go to produce "soft" findings about what might or might not happen.

Here's what is still missing in the science and art of marketing research. First, a general agreement on how to measure the impact of advertising. Second, a method to really predict new product success, especially for new high-tech products. Third, a generalized body of knowledge—which means the right techniques are used for the right reasons (i.e., don't put numbers in a focus group report). A strong link between college training and business techniques is also missing, as is a level of training for that important segment of the industry which provides all the raw data for marketing research: the data collection industry (no one teaches this).

It would be a wonderful step, if at marketing research graduate programs, there were a program developed to collect, synthesize and disseminate such knowledge.

Good advertising works. And good marketing research can help that advertising work even better.

About the Author

J im Nelems has been in marketing research for almost forty years: first with a major consumer packaged goods manufacturer, then with a major advertising agency, and for the last 30 years, as president of his own research firm, The Marketing Workshop Inc., which he founded in 1972 and Compass Marketing Research, a data collection facility he founded in 1982.

Jim is a passionate researcher who really does love taking home a set of tables and deciphering what they mean. Using the dual skills of a detective and a lawyer, but without the bias that might come from working one side of the case versus the other, Jim is able to draw insights and conclusions from the data that might not be so obvious to the casual observer.

And over those many years, Jim has seen hundreds of research studies in which he has wanted to scream and say, "Do they really know what they are talking about?

How could they possibly draw that conclusion? Not only is the conclusion wrong, the real conclusion is exactly opposite from what the report says." He no longer says "this is the worst study I have ever seen," because he knows another one will come along later.

Jim's challenge is to make sure that none of his research reports break any of the 25 secret rules of marketing research. Because he does in fact know what they are.

(Jim lives in Norcross, Georgia, with the rest of his marketing research family: wife Doris who is the company's CFO, daughter Sherri Taylor who is Senior Research Manager, son-in-law Scott Taylor who manages Compass Marketing Research, son David Nelems who as Chief Technical Officer founded a spin off research firm called ActiveGroup, and daughter-in-law Janelle Polito Nelems who is a Senior Qualitative Manager.